FATAL
CHOICE

FATAL CHOICE

NUCLEAR WEAPONS AND THE ILLUSION OF MISSILE DEFENSE

Richard Butler

Westview
PRESS
A Member of the Perseus Books Group

Westview Press books are available at special discounts for bulk purchases in the United States by corporations, institutions, and other organizations. For more information, please contact the Special Markets Department at The Perseus Books Group, 11 Cambridge Center, Cambridge MA 02142, or call (617) 252-5298.

Published in 2001 in the United States of America by Westview Press, 5500 Central Avenue, Boulder, Colorado 80301–2877, and in the United Kingdom by Westview Press, 12 Hid's Copse Road, Cumnor Hill, Oxford OX2 9JJ

Find us on the World Wide Web at www.westviewpress.com

Cataloging-in-Publication Data record available at the Library of Congress.
ISBN 0-8133-4097-7
The paper used in this publication meets the requirements of the American National Standard for Permanence of Paper for Printed Library Materials Z39.48–1984.

10   9   8   7   6   5   4   3   2   1

*This book is dedicated to former
prime minister of Australia Paul Keating, and
his foreign minister, Gareth Evans, in recognition
of their wisdom and courage in establishing,
in 1995, the Canberra Commission on the
Elimination of Nuclear Weapons.*

CONTENTS

Tables and Figures   *ix*
Preface   *xi*
Acknowledgements   *xvii*

  1 The Problem of Nuclear Weapons   1
  2 Arms Control and Security   19
  3 The Non-Proliferation Regime   45
  4 Proliferation Today   75
  5 Nuclear Defense   95
  6 Nuclear Security   121
  7 Plan of Action   139

Notes   157
References   163
Index   167

TABLES AND FIGURES

Tables

2.1 Major arms control treaties and agreements 25

2.2 Current nuclear-weapon state arsenals 31

2.3 Bilateral U.S.-U.S.S.R./Russian nuclear
weapon treaties 36

2.4 Current undeclared nuclear-weapon state arsenals 41

Figures

2.1 U.S. and U.S.S.R./Russian nuclear stockpiles,
1945–2000 29

PREFACE

It will soon be sixty years since nuclear weapons entered human history. In that time, they have been used in war twice; there have been innumerable instances of their possible accidental detonation and repeated false warnings of missile launches; and plans for their use in specific conflicts have been put in motion on at least four occasions. For some fifty of those sixty years, the threat of a nuclear strike has been proffered as the mainstay of international peace and security. Indeed, this posture has been dignified by a doctrine of deterrence—the threat, in the case of the United States and Russia, of mutual assured destruction.

There is little, if anything, in human history to compare with the enormity of what has been at stake in, or the bitter contradiction of, the notion that the preservation of civilization can be assured by the threat of the use of weapons that could destroy life as we know it and the planetary environment that supports it. Nothing compares to the age of nuclear weapons, our age.

Nations and publics have reacted to this extraordinary set of circumstances in two main ways. The nations locked into the nuclear matrix have struggled, on the one hand, to match the nuclear weapon–based power of their perceived adversary—an action that resulted in the number of nuclear weapons in existence growing from the original three to some 80,000—while pledging, on the other hand, to work toward their elimination.

Attitudes among concerned citizens around the world have ranged from an initial extreme existential anxiety in response to the original development and testing of nuclear weapons—leading, for example, to nuclear attack drills and bomb shelters in schools—to the current widespread combination of resignation to the permanent presence of nuclear weapons and a numb distancing from the dangers they pose. This latter attitude includes a classic attitude of denial—the underlying idea that nuclear weapons threaten others rather than us—and an associated uncritical belief in the reliability of nuclear deterrence. The truth is that notwithstanding the pledges by governments, made for some thirty years, to eliminate nuclear weapons and the unstated but palpable wish of very many people that nuclear weapons would simply go away, they continue to exist and threaten all.

There must be no mistake about the threat posed by these weapons. As long as nuclear weapons exist, the possibility that they will be used, either by accident or design, is real. Any use of them would be devastating—literally, politically, and morally. It is also axiomatic that as long as any state possesses nuclear weapons, others, including non-state actors, terrorists, will seek to acquire them. And as the number of those possessing nuclear weapons increases, so does the likelihood of their use.

This book has been written at a special time. We are now in a period in which restraints on the proliferation of nuclear weapons are being seriously challenged. Policies that purport

to respond to these disturbing facts by building a national defense screen are now being implemented by the United States.
These policies fail utterly to address the causes of the proliferation of nuclear weapons, but instead hold the prospect of both
failing to provide defense and increasing the scope of the very
problem they are supposed to solve.

The outrage committed by terrorists against the United
States on September 11, 2001, has made even more urgent
the need to eliminate, once and for all, the threat posed by
nuclear weapons. It has also starkly exposed the illusion of
missile defense.

On September 11, terrorists chose to convert civilian aircraft
into missiles and die delivering them. This choice of weapon
was not anticipated. The possibility of a further terrorist attack
on New York, following the first attack on the World Trade
Center, on February 26, 1993, was under active consideration
by U.S. security authorities. Those who thought about it, including me,[1] expected that the preferred weapon of terrorist
choice might be chemical or biological or, possibly, nuclear.
Given what has now been revealed of the destruction fanatical
terrorist groups are prepared to deliver, attacks with such
weapons cannot be ruled out.

To prevent such attacks, action must be taken, on a widespread international basis, to stamp out terrorism, as such. The
administration is seeking to develop the cooperation and
means to achieve this goal. It will be a difficult and long term
enterprise but it must be undertaken.

Equally urgent and possibly more basic, is action to deny access by terrorist groups to weapons of mass destruction, above

all, nuclear weapons. This could only be achieved by the adoption of measures of the kind advanced in this book.

A national missile defense system, had it then existed, would not have prevented the attacks of September 11, 2001. To proceed with building such a system now would divert massive resources away from the crucial tasks of eradicating terrorism, securing the U.S. homeland, and preventing the proliferation of weapons of mass destruction, including to terrorist groups.

We must draw the right conclusions from September 11. Failure to do so will condemn us to suffer terror again and possibly in large, nuclear, measure.

In these circumstances, what is required is essentially a choice: to survive nuclear weapons or to be sentenced by them, to remain hostage to their terror, if not be their victim. Survival is manifestly the only civilized choice. For it to be made will require people to demand of their governments that they tackle head-on the problem of nuclear weapons.

This book rests on the conviction that the general public, though resigned to the existence of nuclear weapons, retains an underlying belief that nuclear weapons are deeply dangerous and that it would be best for them to be removed from human life. Concerns about whether this can be done with safety, whether others can be trusted to keep faith with nuclear disarmament agreements, and perhaps particularly whether national security can be ensured without nuclear weapons are equally widespread and real. Such important concerns need to be addressed.

This book addresses these questions and, in doing so, recognizes that, in many ways, the right choice is the harder choice, as is so often characteristic of right choices. It also reflects my personal conviction that when an action is clearly right, the fact that it is difficult to take is no reason for failing to act.

Because of the central role the general public must play in any policy choices of the magnitude involved in dealing with the dangers posed by nuclear weapons, this book is addressed to that public. There are more detailed, more academic, more technical writings available on this subject, indeed voluminously so. This book is not intended to compete with or replace them.

Instead, I assume the existence of an interested, intelligent public that lacks accessible information on a subject that it knows is important—nuclear weapons. That public has often been purposely misled about nuclear weapons by persons who are in control of them and want to retain them. The seductive power of nuclear weapons has been skillfully employed for political, nationalistic, and, too often, hateful purposes.

The public has also been told endlessly that what is crucially at issue with nuclear weapons—national survival on the basis of deterrence and mutual assured destruction—is too complex, too difficult for them to understand. Leaders who should know better have reached for what is often the most cynical of appeals for popular consent—"trust me."

I strenuously reject such obfuscation. It recalls the stance of the medieval Catholic Church, which insisted to ordinary people that only the cognoscenti, the priests and monks, could understand the mysteries of life and death. Their stance rested mightily on the fact that the relevant information was recorded in an ancient language, Latin, to which they had exclusive access. This ended when Gutenberg put the Bible into vernacular.

The choice on nuclear weapons also involves life and death. It can be understood by plain people in plain language. This book seeks to encourage such an understanding.

The specific solution to the problem of nuclear weapons proposed in this book may not be the only or perfect one. It is a practical and achievable one, and it addresses the problem of nuclear weapons directly and globally. Leadership will be crucial, and thus it focuses on the need for the United States to lead the way. There can be no doubt that without American leadership, the problem will not be solved. The exercise of that leadership requires the adoption and articulation by the United States of a clear and comprehensive policy on the control and eventual elimination of nuclear weapons. Such a policy does not exist today.

Because what is proposed in this book is both ambitious and difficult, it would be a leap to expect that any U.S. administration would find it easy to initiate such a new policy without strong public support. But if such public support is to be developed, the issues at stake must first be intelligibly explained and debated. If this book contributes to that process, it will have succeeded.

The choice for survival, and not the fatal choice, might then be made.

ACKNOWLEDGMENTS

My work on and study of nuclear weapons and nuclear arms control began in 1964. The people who helped me and gave me friendship and encouragement are innumerable and from many different parts of the world. I cherish my memories of them, especially of those who have since died, and thank them all for their generosity.

I am particularly grateful to D.A.V. Fischer, former deputy director general of the International Atomic Energy Agency, who in a lifetime's work contributed more than any other person to the vitality of the Nuclear Non-Proliferation Treaty. He and his wife, Dr. Pat Fischer, are modest heroes of decency and civility. I will also always remember Allan McKnight, the first inspector general of the IAEA and a fellow Australian. He gave me strength at a moment of extreme need.

One man, always against the grain, gave me a unique opportunity to work with consequence for Australia and internationally in the field of nuclear arms control—former foreign minister and later governor general of Australia, Bill Hayden. I remain grateful to him and recognize the political risks he took in establishing the role of Australian ambassador for disarmament and then naming me to it.

I am also deeply indebted to the series of Australian officials, at all levels, with whom I worked on nuclear policy in Australia and the wider world for over thirty years. They were diligent in the extreme and relentlessly creative.

The members of the Canberra Commission on the Elimination of Nuclear Weapons deserve recognition for their personal efforts over decades, and in the case of Sir Joseph Rotblat FRS, since the beginning of the age of nuclear weapons, of which he was part, and for what they created as a group in 1995–1996.

Indispensable contributions to the writing of this book were made by Leonardo Arriola, my research associate at the Council on Foreign Relations, and Daisy Joye and Lucinda Watson, two extraordinary young Australian women who worked as interns at the council early in 2001. Leo is now on his way to doctoral studies at Stanford University. The world will hear more of him. Daisy and Lucinda clearly have the world at their feet, as they should.

The initial manuscript was prepared splendidly by Fiona Gosschalk.

This writing project was funded by three generous contributors: the Estee Lauder Philanthropic Fund of the Jewish Communal Fund on behalf of Ronald S. Lauder, the Glickenhaus Foundation, and another who, consistent with his modesty, wishes his support to remain a private matter.

The ability to conduct this work at the Council on Foreign Relations was critical, for which I am deeply grateful to its distinguished president, Leslie H. Gelb.

I am grateful to the editorial staff at Westview Press for their skill and patience.

Finally, I thank my wife and family for their encouragement, especially during the extended periods in which I was away, on the arms control road.

It starts with Einstein. He shows that measurement—measurement, on which the whole possibility of science depends—measurement is not an impersonal event that occurs with impartial universality. It's a human act, carried out from a specific point of view in time and space, from the one particular viewpoint of a possible observer. Then, here in Copenhagen in those three years in the mid-twenties we discover that there is no precisely determinable objective universe. That the universe exists only as a series of approximations. Only within the limits determined by our relationship with it. Only through the understanding lodged inside the human head.

—**Niels Bohr in Act II of** *Copenhagen,*
a play by Michael Frayn, 1998

The Problem of
Nuclear Weapons

Three years ago, I took a rest stop at Bombay, now according to the canons of Hindu nationalism renamed Mumbai. I was en route to New York, via Australia, from talks in Baghdad, held in my capacity as chairman of the UN Special Commission to disarm Iraq. I had chosen to stop in India because of my long engagement with and affection for Indian culture. I would have only one day, but I had thought that even a brief contact with the architecture, sounds, colors, and food of India would refresh my enduring affair with one of the greatest of human cultures. The talks in Baghdad had been hostile and tense. This heightened my expectations of my one day of indulgence in India.

As I waited for my bag at the luggage carousel in the airport, I already felt the excitement of arrival. I was there, at last, in India, after an absence of some five years. My reverie was broken by a voice off to one side—"You are that wretched Butler."

I looked around and saw an Indian man approaching me, pointing at me angrily. He was well dressed, forty-something, and apparently sober. My immediate thought was that I was about to get the "why are you persecuting the poor Iraqis" speech, once again. It proved to be not as simple as that.

"Why are you so hateful of India," he demanded. I asked him what he had in mind and got my answer—the Comprehensive Nuclear Test Ban Treaty.

Almost two years earlier, as Australian ambassador to the United Nations, in New York, I had tabled the treaty text in the General Assembly, where it had been adopted overwhelmingly. This had defeated India's earlier blockage of the treaty in Geneva and had involved several very public clashes between me and senior Indian officials. These actions had been widely publicized in India, including newspaper and television pictures of me as the main antagonist of India.

I tried to explain to the man that I was not an enemy of India, quite the opposite. That was why I was in Mumbai, on my own time, with no official duties.

He then explained to me, in terms as clear as any professional negotiator, that it was deeply wrong that the United States, for example, could insist that nuclear weapons were essential to the preservation of its security but refuse to allow the same to India.

"Are we not threatened?" he asked. "We have a long border with China. It has nuclear weapons. It has attacked India in the past. It has occupied Tibet. Why should we not be able to defend ourselves against China?"

I told him that the test ban treaty was a part of measures to control and eventually eliminate all nuclear weapons,

something I had understood all Indian leaders since Ma-
hatma Gandhi had supported. It was not directed against
India, as such.

It was, of course, a touch fatuous to think that this airport argument would lead anywhere or solve anything. Indeed, my
bag had by then arrived, and I wanted to be on my way into the
city. Its end was, however, determined by my new friend.

"I will not be detaining you any further. I am not a ruffian.
But you must know that this nuclear colonialism will not stand.
India's security is as important as America's. We fought for our
independence from the British just as America did. We will defend it."

In response to my last question, he said he was a shopkeeper,
selling textiles and fine saris. The world he saw from his store-
front had indelible features, including historic inequity between sovereign states. The latest form of this was expressed in
ownership of nuclear weapons.

In addition to its enduring interest in reproduction and the
complex urges it engenders, humankind has shown and
recorded a similarly deep interest in seeking to understand
and, more important, characterize the period of history in
which it is presently living. Both impulses search for the meaning of human life and seek to affirm it. The most recurrent
characterization of history is that of modernism—the claim that
our stage of development is the most advanced, the most
evolved and that, specifically, we are liberated from the ignorance and error that shackled those who came before.

The contention that the stage in which we currently find ourselves is modern is factual. How could it be otherwise? That this

self-evident truth is repeated, as a mantra, and infused with finality reveals both a deep inner need and a damaging error.

That inner need is to replace chaos or confusion with order. The error is that of passivity. These impulses are manifested in the attempts, repeated perennially, to identify an organizing principle of history.

On the biological level, an example of this is the Darwinian conceptualization of natural selection and survival of the fittest. In the realm of human psychology, there are the competing ideas of the individual-centered development of personality identified by Freud and those of genetic determinism or behaviorism espoused by others such as Hans Eysenck and B. F. Skinner.

Explanations for the puzzling question of why some parts of the world became industrialized and others did not range from emphasis on the role of the climate, hot versus cold, under which different groups of humans have lived, to varying circumstances of access to metals, food, or water. There are also theories about exposure to disease as an explanation for the rise and fall of civilizations and empires.

Marx provided an explanation of history based on economic determinism and social class. Other theories assert that history has been determined by racial differences, the drive to acquire and exercise power, or the balance of military power. Of course, theological explanations for why things are as they are abound and are among the oldest of all explanations for human events and history itself.

The last century came to be dominated by science and the belief in the measurement of everything, following Albert

Einstein, Niels Bohr, and the other inventors of modern physics. This outlook prevails today. Indeed, it has been extended in ways its originators could scarcely have imagined.

Perhaps above all, such theories are often glitteringly wrapped by their protagonists in the most seductive of all overarching rationales—the claim that what is occurring at any given time is simply the outcome of "human nature," a concept that is both the least precisely mapped and the most enduring of historicisms.

Doubtless there are important elements of truth, and certainly fascination, in all such theories. The list just given is minuscule in comparison with the entire catalogue of various interpretations of the meaning of human history. Much more important, however, than the substantive content of such interpretations of history is the major error that this repeated act of interpretation can lead to in practical terms. It is resignation in the face of what is seen to be the inner mechanism of history: the view that there is nothing we can do about certain events, trends, or circumstances *because* they are determined by this mechanism, that this inner mechanism determines our human fate.

Today, this error is on majestic display with respect to the justifications given for the existence of nuclear weapons, devices that have the ability to destroy all human life. It is majestic because all the features of the drive to make order out of chaos are in play: historicism, misrepresentation of facts, passivity, and resignation to our fate. This hardly makes ours the most modern of all times, though obviously it is. It puts us on par with those who insisted to Columbus that the earth is flat, and they were, of course, that era's most modern of gentlemen and scholars.

What is most shocking about the various arguments that conclude that nuclear weapons are a given, embedded in the very nature of things, is that these weapons are the singular human invention capable of destroying the earth and all that lives on it. Our history deserves better than a resignation to them or an acceptance that we are compelled by nuclear weapons to a *danse macabre.*

These speculations about the nature of things also raise, whether intended or not, the fundamental issue of the relationship between science and the public good. This can be summed up in a question: Is the fact that something can be invented and then made reason enough for it to be made? Some argue that the answer is always in the affirmative, but, again, this has not always been the case in practice. Judgments of whether a given technology serves a useful purpose, and whether or not it is ethical, have been key elements in considering the practical applications of research. The crucial connection between scientific possibilities and human values is now at center stage in the debate over the future applications of modern biology and genetics. And it has always been at issue in nuclear science.

The salient facts of nuclear weapons are clear. They do not exist in nature. They were invented by humans. The decisions to make, deploy, and use nuclear weapons are made by individuals. It is possible to decide to do none of these things. The argument that we cannot disinvent what has already been invented is impeccable. It is typically deployed, however, in a

deeply misleading way by implying absolute involuntarism—
that we are compelled to make what we know how to make.
There is no such compulsion. There are abundant examples of
decisions not to make or use dangerous objects or substances
precisely because they are too dangerous.

A crucial example exists in the forty-some countries that
could make nuclear weapons but have decided not to do so and
have promised never to do so under the Nuclear Non-Proliferation Treaty (NPT). One country, South Africa, made nuclear
weapons but later disassembled and destroyed them. South
Africa is now a non-nuclear-weapon state under the NPT. It
clearly knows how to make nuclear weapons; it made them. It
has committed itself never to do so again.

The assertion that nuclear weapons are a permanent, ubiquitous feature of human life is an opinion, not a fact. To represent
it as the latter is deeply misleading. All that can be said, as a
matter of fact, is that they have existed for fifty-six years. It is
also a fact that five of the eight countries that possess them
have formally declared that it is their policy to eliminate them.
The other three are ambiguous on the issue.

An issue on which there is no lack of clarity is the danger
posed by nuclear weapons. Yet, that danger has been continually misrepresented. The key misrepresentation asserts that nuclear weapons simply cause a larger type of explosion than is
typically yielded by conventional explosives. This is wrong in a
number of important ways.

Nuclear weapons do not simply produce an explosion. They
also release radioactivity, the human and environmental consequences of which are enduring and devastating. From the

beginning of their development until today, the owners of nuclear weapons have sought to at least obscure, and in some instances deny and hide, this fact.

Because of their enormous power, nuclear weapons have become the subject of an arms race. States have acquired greater numbers of more powerful nuclear weapons in the belief that this will assure other states that a nuclear attack would be met by a devastating response. This posture of deterrence, it is argued, ensures that nuclear weapons will not be used. Their only use, at Hiroshima and Nagasaki, which notably was against a non-nuclear-weapon state, occurred when nuclear deterrence was not yet relevant.

It must be recognized that deterrence is and remains a theory, the truth of which necessarily has only a negative proof—that an event did not occur. This is hardly a sound basis for the long-term management of life. It would be more than a pathetic conclusion to the organization of human affairs if, one day, we had to admit that the theory had been wrong. This would not be a merely intellectual moment. It would be a disaster.

There have been, and are today, arms races in conventional weapons, and those hold dangers, too. In pointing this out, the apologists for nuclear weapons sometimes remark that it does not matter much to a person how they are killed, just that they are or are not. Even this bitter observation is not true. To die slowly of radiation sickness is to die a particular death that would matter to that affected person.

Apart from their hard-nosed, realist tenor, such statements seek to draw attention away from the mass destructive, indiscriminate, and radioactive capability of nuclear weapons, which ensure that their use would bring death and damage on a far wider and more enduring scale than conventional weapons. This mass destructive characteristic of nuclear weapons places them in a special category. The line between combatant and non-combatant, which according to both law and principle should be drawn, is removed.

The evolution of the theory of deterrence—of national security based on the maintenance of a specific array and configuration of nuclear weapons—has led to a situation in which the major nuclear-weapon states, the United States and Russia, have put at risk all humankind and the viability of the earth in the name of their own security. The notion that the protection of a given civilization can justify jeopardizing *all* civilization defies logic and should be seen as morally repugnant.

In response to this grave contradiction, the proponents of nuclear-weapon–based national security argue that this threat to all civilization and the planet is greatly exaggerated; they claim that they have it all under control. They point to the safety, communications, and command-and-control systems that have been established for nuclear weapons and their delivery systems, claiming that they are reliable and ensure that the truly dreadful would never happen. They say that the fact that it has not already happened is evidence for the validity of their claim.

The least that could be expected from both the national security standpoint and the public interest is that there would, indeed, be such systems of control, and clearly much has been invested in this being so. This is neither remarkable nor is it a set of circumstances that should attract gratitude.

History re-enters the picture at this point. Does what we know of the past justify faith in such control systems, when the there is so much at stake and the possibility of accident, miscalculation, and criminal or insane behavior is known to be recurrent? Clearly not. Given these facts and the unique and intolerable dangers posed by nuclear weapons, the more rational conclusion would be to seek to address the danger through the removal of nuclear weapons rather than to rely on the idea that control over them will never fail or that there will never be an accident, miscalculation, or terrorists use of them.

There is the contention that there would be danger in the elimination of nuclear weapons, elementally, because of the notion that what has been invented cannot be disinvented, and it would be foolish to think otherwise. The usual extensions of this distressingly passive theory include the following: We might want to dispose of our nuclear weapons, but others may not or may cheat. That is, they might maintain them secretly. Others will always aspire to obtain nuclear weapons, especially rogues or terrorists. We would expose ourselves to great danger, or at least blackmail, if we eliminated our nuclear weapons.

These are real concerns, and the work to address them would be complex, indefinite in duration, and not easily assured of success. But these arguments and concerns fall short of an abiding reality: Absent action by the key nuclear-weapon states to reduce their holdings of nuclear weapons, the impetus for others to acquire the same weapons, and thus increase the overall dangers posed by them, will never decline. In fact, it will grow, as indeed it has in the past and is today.

The problem of nuclear weapons is nuclear weapons. Any serious attempt to address the problems they pose must focus on their very existence. The issues of their control and management are subsidiary. And as long as they exist anywhere, they will spread. The gentleman at Mumbai airport made this clear.

Prevention of that wider dispersal of nuclear weapons—non-proliferation—has been a central goal of the nuclear-weapon states and an overwhelming number of others for thirty years. Work to that end has been remarkably effective, especially given the constant pressures toward proliferation that have existed.

But this non-proliferation objective is by no means secure. Overt proliferation has occurred in Israel, India, and Pakistan, and covert programs for the acquisition of nuclear weapons have been under way in Iran, Iraq, and North Korea. Iraq may already have succeeded in acquiring such a capability. It is to be expected that other countries have either conducted relevant work on nuclear weapons acquisition or are contemplating it. This is to say nothing of the real, but essentially incalculable, order of magnitude of possible acquisition of nuclear weapons by terrorist groups.

These dangers need to be addressed. The vital question is by what means. The choices range from political and technical work to strengthen proliferation controls and make them universal on one end of the spectrum to military action to remove weapons development facilities on the other, or a combination of these measures.

An approach to this task is suggested later in this book. What is important at this point is to identify the problem of the further proliferation of nuclear weapons. It demands a solution.

At root is a debate about whether control over proliferation is possible and, if so, to what degree. Or, if it is not, then is the solution, as the United States now intends, to build new measures of defense against nuclear weapons?

Control over the spread of nuclear weapons can be achieved. The means of control are available. These include restrictions over access to the relevant materials and technologies, inspection and other means of monitoring relevant activities, and the political and legal instruments to clarify ambiguous situations and remedy transgressions of non-proliferation norms if so required. Such control can be exercised if it is decided to do so, with determination.

Preventing the proliferation of nuclear weapons is supported by the overwhelming majority of states. By their actions, these states refrain from acquiring nuclear weapons themselves and seek to ensure through their relations with others, as in export controls, that proliferation does not occur.

What has been less reliable is the willingness of the nuclear-weapon states to take action toward both reducing their arsenals and preventing proliferation, by denying access by others to nuclear-weapons technology and materials as well as enforcing non-proliferation norms.

If the nuclear-weapon states fail to act in these ways, nuclear weapons will undoubtedly proliferate. A specific expression of this failure is the claim, principally made by advocates for the construction of defenses against the newly acquired missile and nuclear-weapons capabilities of other states, that the non-proliferation arrangements are unreliable and cannot be verified, and therefore defensive action must be taken.

The resignation involved in this assertion is extreme. It implies that a law of cheating is both given and insuperable. But there is no such law, especially with respect to our purported impotence in the face of criminal behavior. What is at issue are actions and decisions that are entirely possible and lie within the reach of the actors involved. States can decide to break the rules and acquire nuclear weapons or not, and others can decide to prevent it or remedy proliferation as it occurs or not. None of this is written in the stars or dictated by an iron law of history or "human nature." It is all within the ability of humankind, of real people.

The idea of defending against threats, whether those imposed by missiles and nuclear weapons or by other sources, has a clear basis in logic and law. The former requires little explanation; the latter is codified both nationally and internationally.

In the case of nuclear weapons, however, the decision to build a national defensive shield raises serious issues, apart from the obviously enormous ones of the effectiveness of such a shield and its cost in both absolute and relative terms. These other fundamental issues reveal the elemental view of the world of nuclear weapons—the paradigm—that is in play.

The established paradigm, to which the United States has previously given assent, can be summarized in the following terms. Nuclear weapons deeply threaten national security and international stability. The United States must therefore take action on three fronts: (1) maintain a quantity and quality of nuclear weapons able to deter their use against the United States, that is, a nuclear deterrent capability directed principally, although not exclusively, at Russia; (2) ensure that the threat posed by nuclear weapons does not expand through the emergence of new nuclear-weapon states or nuclear-armed terrorism, and for this purpose, strongly support the NPT and associated agreements; and (3) reduce the size of the problem through arms control and disarmament agreements. In the latter context, the United States would work toward the elimination of nuclear weapons as the overall solution, a commitment required of all nuclear-weapon states as a mainstay of the non-proliferation treaty.

A new paradigm is now being asserted in the context of the proposed national missile defense system. It maintains that non-proliferation arrangements are no longer reliable, and it remains silent on any policy designed to address this concern. It calls for the building of defenses against the newly acquired weapons capability by rogue states and for further reductions in the strategic nuclear weapons of both Russia and the United States, but it is silent on the issue of elimination of nuclear weapons, even though that has been the declared policy of all administrations up to the present one. The United States will continue to rely on nuclear weapons as the fundament of its national security.

This new paradigm expresses resignation from the job of strengthening non-proliferation arrangements, and it attempts to assign the blame for this to the treaties themselves, as if they had a life of their own—claiming that they are "hopelessly flawed." This resignation ensures that they remain flawed and places the specific protection of U.S. security vastly above any action by the United States to alter the security or threat environment. In fact, this paradigm abandons the U.S. commit-

ment to the eventual elimination of nuclear weapons and signals instead a national policy of indefinite reliance on nuclear
weapons for protecting the security of the United States.

The United States is not alone among the nuclear-weapon
states in proclaiming a commitment to the elimination of nuclear weapons while plainly behaving in the opposite direction.
This hypocrisy on the part of the nuclear-weapon states is proving to be extremely dangerous. It will ultimately fail.

The major predictable outcome of this paradigm shift in the
thinking of the U.S. administration is to ensure that the dire
circumstances cited as its justification, the clear outlines of
which are only imprecisely discernible, will become a palpable
reality. Existing nuclear-weapon states, particularly Russia and
China, will not accept that the new U.S. defensive shield will
have no impact on them. They will build new nuclear weapons
in response. The states already on the way to acquiring nuclear
weapons will continue down that path, possibly assisted by nuclear-weapon states, and they will be joined by others. The
world will enter a new period of nuclear weapons development—a second nuclear arms race. It will do this because the
strongest power, the United States, declared itself too weak,
selfish, or frightened.

No amount of insistence by the U.S.-firsters that the United
States has the right and duty to defend itself—that there are
bad and dishonest people in the world who want nuclear
weapons and intend to harm the United States—will alter the
fact that by refusing the choice of detailed and committed work
to address truly difficult circumstances, the harder choice, the
United States will have ensured the realization of its own night-

mare. Current proposals to build a new American fortress will assign to nuclear weapons enduring value and will spur others to adopt the same stance.

The better solution to the real problems posed by the admittedly great pressure under which the non-proliferation regime is straining would be for the United States to lead by making a clear, determined choice. It should refuse to accept the proliferation of nuclear weapons and demonstrate that refusal through the following actions: Engage Russia in a major reduction in the strategic nuclear weapons held by both the United States and Russia and then bring the other nuclear-weapon states into the process of reductions; cancel the Cold War–era states of hair-trigger alerts and the targeting of strategic nuclear weapons; commit major resources to strengthening proliferation controls; and bring into existence a reliable international means of enforcing nuclear non-proliferation norms.

Research on defense against ballistic missiles could continue. As already observed, logic and law sanction such efforts. But a unilateral decision to deploy such a system should not be made unless it becomes clear that others will not join the United States in dealing directly with the threat of nuclear weapons. If the United States does find a reliable way to defeat the threat of ballistic missiles, it should examine the question of how this technology could best serve global safety and stability—by solely national deployment or by deployment shared with others.

For the United States to take such an approach would possibly require another paradigm shift—a shift in a prevailing outlook within the United States—that muscularity always triumphs, that national, or self-centered, decisions are the best and only reliable ones, and that the United States, as the greatest power since the end of the Cold War, should use that power for its own self-interests.

The hardest job of leaders in a democracy is to lead rather than to follow. De Tocqueville reflected on this when he warned of the possible "tyranny of the masses" in the new America he brilliantly observed. U.S. leaders are now called to possibly the largest challenge they have ever confronted. It is to lead ordinary Americans to an understanding that a world in which unilateral action can rule does not exist, even for the greatest power modern history has seen. Perhaps such a world existed for imperial Rome. However, the globalization of our economy, technology transfer, and new advances in communication, which are the key features of our time, prevent the existence of such a world today and in the future.

America's actions, in the years immediately ahead, on the burning question of what to do about nuclear weapons will determine the safety and survival of the world. If the United States uses its extraordinary power in ways freed from the commonplace constraint of narrowly defined self-interest, it will shape the new world, of which it remains the enduring symbol, and turn all past history of the uses of great power on its ear. It will demonstrate, for the first time, that such power can be used to benefit all. And, a world saved from nuclear weapons would strengthen, not weaken, the security of the United States.

This is the choice America can make. It will make such a choice if it is great. In his farewell address, which subsequently became known as his "military-industrial complex" speech,

President Dwight D. Eisenhower said, "Disarmament, with mutual honor and confidence, is a continuing imperative. Together we must learn how to compose differences, not with arms, but with intellect and decent purpose."[1]

His words, spoken forty years ago, have even greater meaning in today's world, threatened as it is by weapons far more devastating than any he had known.

2

Arms Control
and Security

For two years, 1997–1998, I led the United Nations' effort to remove Saddam Hussein's weapons of mass destruction—nuclear, chemical, biological, and the missiles to deliver them. After the Gulf War, the UN Security Council had directed that those weapons be "destroyed, removed, or rendered harmless." There was nothing unclear about it. The Security Council's decisions are binding in international law. Saddam had such weapons or, in the case of nuclear weapons, was building them. He had already used some of them, including on the Iraqi people. My job was to find the weapons and destroy them.

This took me to Baghdad almost a dozen times. The man Saddam had put in charge of dealing with me, or more pertinently of ensuring that our work did not succeed, was Deputy Prime Minister Tariq Aziz. My meetings in Baghdad were with him and the team of Iraqi generals who ran Saddam's weapons programs. When I went out into the field, I was shepherded by one of them. Given Baghdad and Iraq's antiquity and place in biblical history, I would often ask myself, in conjunction with particular events, which part of the Bible would apply here. During one trip to a field outside Baghdad, where we were searching for missile parts, I was accompanied by the Iraqi general in charge of missiles, Amer Rashid. It put me in mind of the biblical reference to "lambs led to the slaughter." Incidentally, the weapons-of-mass-destruction industry in Iraq is something of a family business. Rashid's wife, Rihab Rashida Taha, was the lead scientist in Iraq's biological weapons program. She was once referred to in a British newspaper as "Dr. Germ." The British would know; she trained for her Ph.D. there.

Whether I was dealing with Aziz, Rashid, or any of the others in Baghdad, one figure was always present in the shadows— Saddam. These were clearly his weapons. He saw them as critical to his power both within Iraq and beyond. He knew about the weapons in detail and personally directed which particular biological cocktail, for example, should be mixed. He richly rewarded the scientists (and their families) who worked on the weapons, or threatened their lives if they did not perform to his requirements, and he delivered on those threats. Those who work for him benefit from it richly, but they are deeply afraid of him—with good reason.

The determination his representatives displayed, the language used, the signals sent, led me to the concept of obsession or addiction to explain Saddam's attitude toward the deadliest of weapons. Simply, he is addicted to weapons of mass destruction.

This is intrinsically alarming, but even more alarming is another conclusion I reached, one that has to do with moral sensibility, not weapons. Saddam and his regime do not believe that there is anything wrong with their addiction.

On one occasion in 1997, I had a lengthy and agitated discussion with Lt. General Amer Al Sa'adi, scientific adviser to Saddam and overall director of the biological weapons program. I had pressed him hard on the transparent nonsense he had put to my team of biological inspectors on aspects of Iraq's programs. Toward the end of our conversation, he reached for a new explanation for what he claimed was the minor size and nature of Iraq's program. He said they had lacked Ph.D.'s. If they had had more properly qualified scientists, they would have been able to build a bigger and better program. He said all this with more than a touch of regret, of "if only."

I will never know whether this was theater—there was an abundance of that—but when I next met Aziz, with Al Sa'adi present, I decided to take it seriously. I complained strongly. "This man," I said, "has actually sat in front of me and lamented, cried tears, about the fact that you lacked the necessary resources to build a large biological weapons program. It's outrageous!"

Aziz plainly indicated that he did not understand my point. He asked me to make clearer what I was getting at. When I repeated my point, making clear that biological weapons are illegal, he dismissively said, "Oh, that point. Well, Al Sa'adi was right. We would have."

I do not suggest that anyone should be surprised at Aziz and Al Sa'adi's attitude. They are the willing servants of a regime, the currency of which is homicide. What is at issue is far deeper: a view of national interest and national security that asserts that any means is justifiable if it protects that interest, that security. Such an answer to the ancient question of the relationship between ends and means requires the dismissal of other concerns of a moral character, such as whether weapons based on germs or mass destruction should be admissible in civilized society. They are dismissed in Baghdad today. Thankfully, they are not in most of the world.

The problem Iraq presents today has its origin, indelibly, in the nature of its present government. That may not change in the foreseeable future, but the specific questions on the relationship between security of the state and weapons, which are so starkly and distortedly raised in the case of Iraq, are abiding ones to which arms control can provide an important part of the answer.

The belief that weapons play a central role in the provision of security to the state, the village, the clan, or the individual is ancient. The elemental form of this belief—that those armed with stronger weapons will prevail in a conflict—extends from the lowest level, on the street where the handgun will typically defeat the knife, to the highest level, where opposed nation-states are armed with the most advanced weapons technology can provide.

Arguments against this belief have always failed, no matter to what higher moral or other authority people opposed to particular weapons have appealed. Indeed, the development of theologically approved doctrines of the just war or holy war have tended to nullify the effect of appeals to higher sources of reason or morality in support of disarmament. This is to say nothing of the not uncommon phenomenon of wars waged in the name of religion, even though the religion being defended or advanced has, as one of its tenets, the virtually universal principle of opposition to homicide. On the whole, organized religion, as against religious individuals, has demonstrated little moral consistency on the issues of arms, war, or peace.

The long history of arms control agreements is marked by repeated failure, especially when the objective sought has been outright disarmament. From among the very many arguments that this history has engendered, two questions are particularly recurrent: Does the existence of weapons cause conflict, or does the occurrence of conflict drive acquisition of weapons? Is it in the basic nature of humankind to always search for the better weapon?

Most people who think about these questions usually arrive at broadly similar answers. The human nature explanation for the perpetual interest of people or groups in ever better weapons is popular, especially among those who are deeply skeptical of arms control of any kind, let alone disarmament, which they, not unexpectedly, loathe. They also typically insist that "weapons don't make war, humans do," thus sidelining entirely the obvious role that the existence and nature of weapons have upon the calculation of threat and hostility. For their various reasons, these individuals either give up on arms control or oppose it, citing their philosophic convictions.

In contrast to this somber, pessimistic background, the record of increasing recourse to arms control as a means of improving the management of security has been an evolving one, especially as what proved to be a very bloody twentieth century proceeded.

Early attempts in the modern period to advance arms control arrangements, beginning at The Hague Peace Conferences in 1899 and 1907, were widely supported. Technological developments at the turn of the century were seen increasingly as leaving civilians intolerably vulnerable to the destructive power of modern warfare. Although the Hague treaties were violated during World War I, they provided both a moral norm and a legal standard against which offenders could be judged.

The use of chemical weapons during World War I was understood therefore by all sides to be a violation of what constituted civilized conduct. And, instead of allowing the original prohibition against chemical weapons to collapse, the international community sought to institutionalize further the norm in the 1925 Geneva Protocol outlawing the use of asphyxiating and poisonous gases in warfare. This has now been overtaken, for most purposes, by the much more extensive Chemical Weapons Convention of 1993. Most important, the underlying principle involved in the Geneva Protocol—some weapon types are not admissible in civilized society—has grown in strength and has been extended to the nuclear and biological weapons fields.

Following World War II and the emergence of nuclear weapons, the conviction that certain classes of weapons should be banned or should be excluded from certain environments—identified areas of the earth, the seas, the skies, and space—has led to the development of a range of arms control treaties, most of which have proven to be broadly effective. Table 2.1 provides a list of key extant multilateral treaties covering nuclear, chemical, biological, and other major weapon types.

TABLE 2.1   Major Arms Control Treaties and Agreements

Multilateral Nuclear Weapon Treaties

05 Aug 1963	Limited Test Ban Treaty
14 Feb 1967	Tlatelolco Treaty on Nuclear Weapons in Latin America
01 Jul 1968	Treaty on the Non-Proliferation of Nuclear Weapons (NPT)
06 Aug 1985	South Pacific Nuclear Free Zone Treaty (Rarotonga Treaty)
11 May 1995	Indefinite Extension of NPT
15 Dec 1995	Bangkok Treaty on the Southeast Asia Nuclear-Weapon-Free Zone
11 Apr 1996	Pelindaba Treaty on the Nuclear-Weapon-Free Zone in Africa
10 Sep 1996	Comprehensive Nuclear Test-Ban Treaty°

Chemical, Biological, and Other Major Weapon Treaties

17 Jun 1925	Geneva Protocol
10 Apr 1972	Biological Weapons Convention
10 Dec 1976	Environmental Modification Convention
13 Jan 1993	Chemical Weapons Convention
03 Dec 1997	Ottawa Convention Banning Landmines

°Not yet entered into force.
SOURCE: UN Department for Disarmament Affairs, US Arms Control and Disarmament Agency, and Federation of American Scientists.

The current track record of the international community on arms control and disarmament agreements demonstrates a larger reliance on such agreements than in virtually any prior period. The question of why this has proven to be the case deserves examination. At least four reasons can be identified.

- The wars of the twentieth century saw the emergence of weapons with unprecedented destructive capability.
- The prevalence of war has increased, bringing death and destruction on a previously unimagined scale.
- The massive cost of modern weapons makes an arms race prohibitive for most nations.

- Nations have recognized that unchecked arms races could have no end in terms of challenges to the management of both security and resource costs.

There may be other reasons, beyond these highly practical ones, for the upsurge in arms control agreements during the past fifty years. It would be comforting to think that a value or ethics-based judgment was in play, but there is only scattered evidence for the existence of that motivation on the level of governments.

What seems to have occurred is that at least a partial revision of the perennial philosophy alluded to here—that the stronger weapon is always the better one—has engendered the effect that some weapons are viewed as so dangerous that national security is enhanced if arrangements can be made for their general control rather than for their acquisition.

This notion, which I term the *replacement phenomenon,* that is, the replacement of weapons acquisition by arms control arrangements, has become an emerging characteristic of the age of weapons of mass destruction. Its motivation is the traditional one—protection of national security—but its behavioral manifestation, *replacement,* is relatively novel. It would be a mistake, however, to paint a rosy picture of this development. At least three facts make this so.

First, deep suspicion remains in most relevant circles about whether arms control agreements can be verified or relied upon. This very real problem will be discussed further.

Second, in the same circles, there is profound discomfort with a departure from the traditional concept of national security—the view that it is human nature to seek ever better weapons. A derived assumption of this thinking is that any opponent thinks exactly as you do. What is at work here is the timeless unease about any change in long-established patterns of thought for which, it is argued, history produces a legion of justifying examples. These instincts remain strong and argue in favor of acquiring ever better weapons rather than relying on arms control.

Third, even if there are rules, it should be kept in mind that these arms control solutions are relatively new and engender all of the feelings of insecurity flowing from the simple fact of novelty.

There is also deep anxiety about the possible existence of states that will cheat on arms control agreements—the rogue state in today's terminology. This is a source of insecurity different from those just mentioned because the problem of verification of compliance with arms control agreements is a systemic one, and the rogue state is inherently extrasystemic. The question that nags is, if we stay our hand on weapons acquisitions, will we then be exposing ourselves to great danger from the rogue that has not stayed its own?

There is perhaps one other related thought process derived from these more evident ones—the idea that arms control is good, provided it controls the arms of others, but not ours. This may, on the face of it, seem an absurd, obviously unsustainable proposition, but there is repeated evidence for its existence. The now established attitude of the nuclear-weapon states toward the NPT—that it is essentially designed to control non-nuclear-weapon states rather than all states—is a key example.

A few central realities can be highlighted from these facts about the current arms control climate. There is broad recognition that arms control arrangements can enhance national security, if they are reliably arranged. This proviso on their reliability is a major matter of substance, but the potentially positive effect of arms control arrangements on national security, especially with respect to weapons of mass destruction, is acknowledged.

Basic to this outlook is recognition that the destructive power of weapons of mass destruction has transformed the security landscape. The challenge they pose to security cannot be met by traditional responses, the main one of which is competition in arms. So, even if dragged kicking and screaming against their established instincts to the arms control task, national governments have increasingly accepted that it is in their interest to engage in it.

In spite of the profound dangers produced by the Cold War, many consider that it did provide a certain predictability in the management of international relations and that this was in itself a source of security, which has now been lost. Whatever the truth of this speculation, it is the case that beginning in the 1970s, the United States and the Soviet Union assessed that the nuclear balance was becoming increasingly complex and needed to be better managed in the interests of their individual national security.

As a consequence, a series of agreements was negotiated to provide for ceilings on strategic systems, the elimination of some intermediate range systems, the removal of short-range battlefield weapons, and communications arrangements designed to ensure that accidental launches of missiles carrying nuclear warheads could be immediately signaled to the other side, thus putting off retaliatory action.

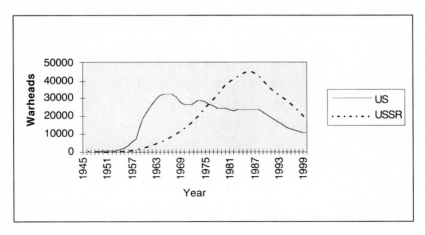

FIGURE 2.1 U.S. and U.S.S.R./Russian Nuclear Stockpiles, 1945–2000

The status of U.S. and Soviet/Russian nuclear weapon holdings from 1945 to the present is charted in Figure 2.1.

The perceived need for a greater degree of safety also led both sides, early in the 1970s, to develop anti-ballistic missile (ABM) systems. When it was recognized, subsequently, that such systems might lead to a greater uncertainty in the reliability of nuclear deterrence, an agreement was negotiated between the United States and the Soviet Union limiting the extent to which each side could deploy anti-ballistic missile defense systems. This was established in the ABM Treaty of 1972, which limited the number of anti-ballistic missile deployment sites and early-warning systems each side could maintain and restricted qualitative or technological improvements to those systems. The treaty was hailed as an important contribution to the maintenance of strategic stability.

Parallel with the arms control developments between the United States and the Soviet Union, the three other nuclear-weapon states continued building their nuclear weapons to meet their own perceived national security needs. The systems built by the United Kingdom, France, and China were considerably smaller than those developed by the two major protagonists. Their nuclear arsenals contained hundreds rather than thousands of nuclear weapons mounted in a variety of configurations and platforms. In the cases of the United Kingdom and France, their capabilities were designed to protect their own homelands and rested on the assumption that global nuclear deterrence would be essentially maintained by the United States and the Soviet Union.

The purpose of China's nuclear weapons system has never been as transparent, but what has been clear is that China paid no particular regard to the postures of the United States and the Soviet Union. It has not pretended to be in competition with them. The threat of China's nuclear weapons capability is, however, keenly felt in its region—in Japan, India, and Taiwan in particular—and that threat will grow as China's nuclear weapons development expands.

The present status of the nuclear weapons holdings of the five main nuclear-weapon states is indicated in Table 2.2.

Although the world no longer lives under the ideological struggle of the Cold War, the issue of further reductions in nuclear weapons must continue to be addressed. Both the United States and Russia maintain nuclear weapon stocks vastly in excess of what would be required to assure mutual deterrence. If each were to persist in that posture of deterrence, their national security could be safely maintained with far fewer strategic nuclear weapons on each side. Very simply, they do not need to be able to destroy each other several times over in order to be

TABLE 2.2   Current Nuclear-Weapon State Arsenals

	Strategic Nuclear Weapons	Non-Strategic Nuclear Weapons [1]	Other Nuclear Weapons [2]	Estimated Total Nuclear Weapons
United States	7,206	1,670	~1,000–2,000	~10,500
Russia	5,606	~3,800	~10,000	~20,000
China	290	120		410
France	348			348
United Kingdom	185			185

NOTES: (1) Non-strategic nuclear weapons include tactical and short-range nuclear weapons. (2) The category of Other Nuclear Weapons includes non-deployed weapons awaiting dismantlement and weapons held in reserve for quality assurance, testing, or as a hedge against the possible breakdown in existing arms control arrangements.

SOURCES:

Carnegie Endowment for International Peace. "China Nuclear Forces, 2001." Proliferation News and Resources. Available at http://www.ceip.org/files/nonprolif/numbers/china.as.

—. "France Nuclear Forces, 2001." Proliferation News and Resources. Available at http://www.ceip.org/files/nonprolif/numbers/france.as.

—. "Russia Nuclear Forces, 2001." Proliferation News and Resources. Available at http://www.ceip.org/files/nonprolif/numbers/russia.as.

—. "United Kingdom Nuclear Forces, 2001." Proliferation News and Resources. Available at http://www.ceip.org/files/nonprolif/numbers/uk.as.

—. "United States Nuclear Forces, 2001." Proliferation News and Resources. Available at http://www.ceip.org/files/nonprolif/numbers/us.as.

Center for Defense Information. "Current World Nuclear Arsenals." Available at http://www.cdi.org/issues/nukef&f/database/nukestab.html.

Norris, Robert S., William M. Arkin et al. "Chinese Nuclear Forces." NRDC Nuclear Notebook, Bulletin of Atomic Scientists, November/December 2000. Available at http://www.the-bulletin.org/issues/nukenotes/nd00nukenote.html.

—. "French Nuclear Forces, 2001." NRDC Nuclear Notebook, Bulletin of Atomic Scientists, July/August 2001. Available at http://www.thebulletin.org/issues/nukenotes/ja00nukenote.html.

—. "French and British Nuclear Forces." NRDC Nuclear Notebook, Bulletin of Atomic Scientists, September/October 2000. Available at http://www.thebulletin.org/issues/nukenotes/so00nukenote.html.

—. "Global Nuclear Stockpiles, 1945–2000." NRDC Nuclear Notebook, Bulletin of Atomic Scientists, March/April 2000. Available at http://www.thebulletin.org/issues/nukenotes/ma00nukenote.html.

—. "Russian Nuclear Forces." NRDC Nuclear Notebook, Bulletin of Atomic Scientists, May/June 2001. Available at http://www.thebulletin.org/issues/nukenotes/mj01nukenote.html.

—. "U.S. Nuclear Forces." NRDC Nuclear Notebook, Bulletin of Atomic Scientists, March/April 2001. Available at http://www.thebulletin.org/issues/nukenotes/ma01nukenote.html.

U.S. Department of State. "START I Aggregate Numbers of Strategic Offensive Arms." Fact Sheet, Bureau of Arms Control, 1 April 2001.

secure. A far lower level of nuclear weapons on each side could be agreed to if they took the political decision to reach that agreement. The resulting level of strategic weapons would still allow them to ensure their security against attack from any other source, if the assumptions of deterrence are held to be valid and operative.

The continued maintenance of excessive strategic nuclear weapons inevitably produces challenges to the management of those systems from the standpoints of accident or miscalculation. This is especially the case given that a portion of U.S. and Russian strategic systems continue to be maintained in a state of hair-trigger alert. This Cold War posture has not changed even though those circumstances ended ten years ago.

The cost of maintaining those systems, moreover, is immense. It is estimated that the United States has spent almost $5.5 trillion on nuclear weapons since their first development. Approximately 14 percent of the defense budget, $35 billion, is annually expended on nuclear weapons. This works out to be more than $96 million a day.[1]

Between 1940 and 1996, U.S. federal government spending on nuclear weapons exceeded the combined total spending on education, training, employment, and social services; agriculture; natural resources and the environment; general science and space research; community and regional development (including disaster relief); law enforcement; and energy production and regulation.[2]

A comparable estimate on the Russian side is not available. What is known, however, is that Russia can no longer afford a nuclear arsenal of several thousand strategic warheads. The military's ability to maintain its nuclear weapons systems, especially from the crucial standpoint of safety, has sharply eroded. The danger flowing from this fact, both with respect to the systems as such and from the possibility that Russian nuclear weapons may be sold or given to others, is immense.

An extensive survey conducted in five of Russia's nuclear cities found that deteriorating economic conditions might lead nuclear weapon specialists to feel compelled to sell their services abroad. The survey found that over 62 percent of nuclear specialists earn less than $50 per month; over half are forced to supplement their incomes through second jobs; 14 percent of experts would like to work outside Russia, and 6 percent would be willing to move "any place at all"; and perhaps most worrisome, some 80 percent would be willing to work for a foreign country's military industry.[3]

A state's very possession of nuclear weapons demonstrates the inevitability that if such a state or group believed that its fundamental interests were gravely threatened or compromised, it would use them. That is why they are developed and maintained. And such use could even occur in a futile situation, that is, as a last unsurvivable act. The overall consequences of such a decision would be incalculable.

While nuclear weapons exist, there is also a significant risk that at some point they will be used by accident. Most accidents occur during weapons assembly or storage, loading or ground transportation, or when the nuclear weapons are in their delivery vehicles (such as missiles or aircraft).[4] From 1950 to 1980, in the United States alone, the Department of Defense has officially recorded thirty-two nuclear accidents or incidents.[5] However, the Center for Defense Information (CDI) maintains that this list is incomplete, citing at least fifty-four incidents involving U.S. nuclear weapons during the same period.[6] At least seven of these incidents involved nuclear warheads that were lost either temporarily or permanently, including a 7,600-pound nuclear bomb that has been missing in the sea off the Georgia coast since 1958.[7]

Any use of nuclear weapons would be a catastrophe. It is impossible to calculate accurately the global environmental consequences of the use of nuclear weapons, but the least that can be assessed is that they would be grave and very likely enduring. It is also possible that such use would not be limited to one strike; instead, it would lead to the wider use of weapons and an escalating situation. Moreover, any use of nuclear weapons would involve crossing a political, psychological, and moral threshold, transforming the world as we know it. The idea of a limited use of nuclear weapons for a just purpose, from which all would recover, perhaps older and wiser, is fanciful in the extreme. Much more likely is a reaction of child-like simplicity— "If it was all right for you to act in that way, why can't I?"

The continued existence of nuclear weapons also guarantees that as long as any state has nuclear weapons, others will seek to acquire them. This is the axiom of proliferation, and it is proportionate—the larger the number of nuclear weapons in existence, the stronger will be the pressures toward proliferation. What this amounts to is that the problem with nuclear weapons is their characteristics, not their political or technological origin. The dangers they pose can be addressed only by direct action on the existence of nuclear weapons.

If the nuclear-weapon states continue to fail to meet their obligations, both in international law and in national policy, to work toward the elimination of nuclear weapons, the result will be the breakdown of the structure of nuclear non-proliferation—the NPT, export controls, and limited transfers of technology. This outcome is underway today.

Almost thirty years ago, the United States and the Soviet Union recognized that the problem of nuclear weapons and the nuclear arms race was getting out of hand. They put a stop to that race and began to reduce their weapons holdings. This was achieved through treaties they negotiated and adopted. Their decision to take such action was positive, but it needs to be taken further if the continuing danger is to be removed. The main treaties are listed in Table 2.3.

The present commitment of the United States and Russia to nuclear weapons reductions was made in 1993 under the Strategic Arms Reduction Treaty (START II), which would cut the number of intercontinental ballistic missiles (ICBMs) and multiple-warhead (MIRVed) ICBMs to 3,500 warheads in each country by December 31, 2007. START II was ratified by the U.S. Senate in January 1996 and by the Russian Duma in April 2000. However, the Duma tied a series of conditions to its ratification of START II, including a provision stating that U.S. withdrawal from or violation of the ABM treaty would constitute grounds for Russia's own withdrawal from START II.

An essential first step toward reinvigorating nuclear disarmament would be for both the United States and Russia to implement START II. More useful would be for them to identify a significantly lower number of weapons on each side and to set

TABLE 2.3   Bilateral U.S.-U.S.S.R./Russian Nuclear Weapon Treaties

26 May 1972	Anti-Ballistic Missile Treaty
03 Jul 1974	Threshold Test Ban Treaty
18 Jun 1979	SALT II Treaty
08 Dec 1987	INF Treaty
31 Jul 1991	Strategic Arms Reduction Treaty (START I)
03 Jan 1993	Strategic Arms Reduction Treaty (START II)

SOURCE: UN Department for Disarmament Affairs, US Arms Control and Disarmament Agency, and Federation of American Scientists

in motion a process of reduction down to those levels. Both sides agreed at Helsinki in 1997 to start negotiations on a START III arrangement as soon as Russia ratified START II. The current proposal for START III would reduce the nuclear warheads on each side to between 2,000 and 2,500, but Russia has already formally stated that it would be willing to lower that number to 1,500.

The two sides, however, could go further. The specific number involved in the next round of negotiations could be realistically lower, for example, some 1,000 apiece, or even fewer. In order to determine this number, they would need to be more searching and truthful than on any prior occasion about precisely what was required for their national defense given the assumption that each side retained some nuclear weapons.

The American president could initiate this process by revising the guidelines for targeting U.S. nuclear weapons. Specifically, the president could narrow the parameters that presently define potential nuclear targets. Military planners use the president's guidelines, as set in a presidential decision directive, to calculate the number of warheads required to ensure America's nuclear deterrent capability and to determine target sites in Russia and other potentially threatening countries. This target list forms part of the country's overall strategic war plan, known as the Single Integrated Operational Plan (SIOP).

The targeting guidelines were last revised by President Clinton in November 1997, marking the first change since President Reagan issued his directive in 1981.[8] Although the revised presidential guidelines dropped Reagan's emphasis on winning a prolonged nuclear war—an unlikely outcome under any kind of scenario—they sustain a distinctly Cold War outlook. In fact, the target list has grown by 20 percent.[9] It not only targets traditional sites in Russia, such as military, leadership, and industrial complexes, but now also includes sites in China and other states that might use chemical or biological weapons against the United States.

In this context, a statement made in Moscow by former Secretary of Defense Robert S. McNamara, on the occasion of a review, in May 2001, of the Cuban missile crisis, is relevant:

> As we sit here tonight, you, Russia, have about 6,500 strategic nuclear warheads directed at us, most on hair-trigger alert. We have 7,500 strategic nuclear warheads directed at you, with 2,500 on fifteen-minute alert. On average, each of our warheads has twenty times the destructive power of the Hiroshima or Nagasaki bombs.
>
> Now, as a matter of policy, the United States does not target nuclear weapons at populations, but the last time I checked we had 200 nuclear warheads targeted on Moscow, not on its population, but on its military facilities, command-and-control facilities,

communications centers, military weapons, et cetera. But imagine what 200 warheads, each twenty times more powerful than the Hiroshima bomb, imagine what that would do to Moscow's population of twelve million.

Now, what's the meaning of my statement that 2,500 of our warheads are on fifteen-minute alert? It simply means this: They can be launched within fifteen minutes after we receive warning of a strike on the U.S., before the warheads of that strike hit their targets. . . .

We should accelerate the rate of elimination of offensive weapons. Both [the Russian and U.S. governments] have given some indication they would be willing to move unilaterally toward reducing to, say, 1,500 warheads from the current level of 7,000 or 6,000. We should certainly greatly reduce the risk we face because of this hair-trigger alert, and we should surely move to strengthen the non-proliferation regimes affecting the proliferation of weapons across the world, particularly by rogue states. I think we should work with China and other nuclear powers to strengthen the non-proliferation regime.

The compelling virtue of a low number of nuclear warheads—in addition to greatly reducing the danger deriving from the vastly excessive and superfluous destructive power of even the START II numbers—is that the United States and Russia would be in a position to call the other three nuclear-weapon states to the negotiating table. Each of those states has indicated that it would be prepared to submit its nuclear weapon holdings to reductions once the numbers held by the United States and Russia came closer to those held by them. In

such a setting, the five nations could then proceed toward reductions all around, heading in the direction of the ultimate
elimination of nuclear weapons.

At the beginning of the reduction process, Russia and the
United States could take other actions that would both greatly
increase nuclear safety, especially by avoiding miscalculation or
accident, and signal the earnestness of their intentions to all others. These actions would include de-alerting the systems they
have mutually targeted, ratifying and bringing into force the
Comprehensive Nuclear Test Ban Treaty (CTBT) of 1996, and
negotiating and implementing a treaty banning the further manufacture of weapons-grade fissile material—the "cut-off" treaty.

A key source of resistance to such steps in both Washington
and Moscow is found among those who argue that U.S.-Russ-
ian reductions would increase the relative value of the nuclear
weapons held by the other nuclear-weapon states and, indeed,
of other weapons of mass destruction held by both states and
non-state actors.

This reasoning is misleading, implying as it does that the holding of excessive nuclear weapons capacity by the United States
and Russia in some way deters the proliferation of other
weapons of mass destruction by other states or non-state actors.
In fact, the reverse is true. Although this line of argumentation
is manifestly flawed, to change it would require no less than a
paradigm shift in the mentality that was forged by the Cold War.

The opponents of nuclear arms control and other forms of
weapons of mass destruction (WMD) control argue that the
treaty undertakings involved in such arrangements cannot be
verified. This is a gross exaggeration. Effective verification

methodologies can be constructed. Very often the expressed skepticism with respect to verification is, in fact, a much more justified skepticism about the possibility that any state determined enough to break the rules, as seen in the case of Iraq, will ultimately evade enforcement of those rules. Reliable enforcement of agreed international norms is what is at issue, not reliable verification. The former is harder than the latter, but is required if regimes of WMD control are to be effective.

The same principle applies to the problems posed by the non-NPT nuclear-weapon states—Israel, India, and Pakistan. When the major nuclear-weapon states embark on a process of reducing their nuclear arsenals, they will be in a position to insist that these three states join in the process. Although the outcome of such insistence cannot be predicted, what can be predicted with certainty is that absent any such commitment by the five major nuclear-weapon states, the probability that Israel, India, or Pakistan would take part in any nuclear arms control would be zero. Table 2.4 outlines the holdings of nuclear weapons by the three non-NPT nuclear-weapon states.

As far as the specific case of Israel is concerned, progress with respect to its WMD capability would need to be placed in the political context of a settlement between Israel and Palestine. It would also require wider action to establish the Middle East as a zone free of weapons of mass destruction, as has been committed to by all major powers through Security Council resolutions.

The case of Israel and its nuclear weapons exemplifies clearly the vicious circle forged by nuclear weapons. Israel faces an elemental hostility. Popular sentiment in surrounding countries is that Israel should not exist. Throughout its existence, Israel has

TABLE 2.4   Current Undeclared Nuclear–Weapon State Arsenals

Estimated Total Number of Nuclear Weapons	
Israel	100–200
India	60–80
Pakistan	30–50

SOURCES:

Arms Control Association. "The State of Nuclear Proliferation 2001." Arms Control Association Fact Sheet. Available at http://www.armscontrol.org/factsheets/statefct.asp.

Carnegie Endowment for International Peace. "India." Proliferation News and Resources. Available at http://www.ceip.org/files/nonprolif/numbers/india.as.

—. "Israel." Proliferation News and Resources. Available at http://www.ceip.org/files/nonprolif/numbers/israel.as.

—. "Pakistan." Proliferation News and Resources. Available at http://www.ceip.org/files/nonprolif/numbers/pakistan.as.

Center for Defense Information. "Current World Nuclear Arsenals." Available at http://www.cdi.org/issues/nukef&f/database/nukestab.html.

Federation of American Scientists. "India Nuclear Weapons." Available at http://www.fas.org/nuke/guide/india/nuke/index.html.

—. "Israel Nuclear Weapons." Available at http://www.fas.org/nuke/guide/israel/nuke/index.html.

—. "Pakistan Nuclear Weapons." Available at http://www.fas.org/nuke/guide/pakistan/nuke/index.html.

faced states and groups committed to its elimination. Among its many responses has been its creation of nuclear weapons. But that action has been deployed by Israel's enemies as justification for the acquisition of weapons of mass destruction, including the attempts by Iraq to acquire nuclear weapons. At the level of the "Arab street," there is widespread support for Iraq's weapons of mass destruction acquisition because they are seen as justified by Israel's possession of nuclear weapons.

In my discussions in Baghdad in 1997–1998, I was repeatedly confronted by the double standard involved in our efforts to disarm Iraq, while no such effort was being made with respect to Israel. In a personal conversation with Iraqi Deputy Prime

Minister Tariq Aziz in 1997, he insisted to me that Iraq had felt compelled to create weapons of mass destruction, particularly biological weapons, to counter Israel's nuclear weapons capability.

The genocidal character of what he put to me was sickening, but his arguments on the inequity of the situation others in the region faced with respect to Israel's weapons capability was hard to answer. I sought refuge in the undertaking given by the Security Council that the removal of Iraq's weapons of mass destruction capability would then lead to wider arms control efforts in the Middle East. Aziz was less than convinced.

This is the vicious circle. Israel believes that it needs the protection afforded by nuclear weapons because of the hostility displayed toward it. Its possession of nuclear weapons enlarges that hostility and thus supports it becoming ever more desperately armed.

The circuit breaker will be a political settlement. But, if that is to hold, it will need to be supported by measures of arms control, including measures related to Israel's nuclear weapons capability. This promise must be credible if a settlement is to be reached.

The work involved in reducing nuclear weapons and continuing on the path toward their elimination is daunting. The major obstacle in its way is the widespread view that they have made a singular contribution to national security and that eliminating them might expose us to great danger. This view is heightened by the idea that although the United States, the "good guys," might be prepared to contemplate such a step, other less principled people clearly would not, so the United States would make itself vulnerable and fall victim to their wickedness.

This outlook is not without merit. It certainly has the virtues of relative simplicity, but it bears analysis, precisely because its simplicity is deceptive.

In the first instance, it assumes that nuclear weapons are here to stay. The fact that nuclear weapons exist now and could be made again in the future is irrefutable. That humankind will always make or possess them is not. This would depend on decisions made by people. It is possible to decide to eliminate nuclear weapons and never to reconstitute them.

Because nuclear weapons have been invented and because they are therefore here to stay is both a powerful idea and a prediction. If the attitudes that have sustained nuclear weapons up to the present time persist, this prediction is certain to prove true. But this is more than a prediction. It is also a resignation. It is a refusal to take up an immensely difficult challenge and to recognize dangers that should be deemed unacceptable. It is postponing a problem to future generations, behaving like the ostrich, burying its head in the sand in the belief that avoiding the sight of a threat will remove it.

In the field of nuclear weapons, the posture of the ostrich has widespread support. This is seen in the popular version of the role played by nuclear weapons during the Cold War: Nuclear weapons kept us safe from the Russians. This view involves a massive disconnect between the Cold War as a situation of extreme U.S.-Soviet hostility on the one hand, and the arms race it spawned on the other. There was no such disconnect. An integral part of the Cold War *was* the nuclear arms race. Its threat was represented by nuclear weapons, and it would have been vastly lower had they not existed. Both sides were threatened precisely because they chose to walk down the nuclear weapons path. History did not dictate it to them. Stalin chose this path at Potsdam, on July 24, 1945, immediately after President Harry S. Truman told him about the successful U.S. test detonation at Alamogordo.

That nuclear weapons were never used during the Cold War was remarkable. Whether this was the consequence of good management rather than considerable good fortune is deeply debatable. For instance, it may have been immensely fortunate that John F. Kennedy, rather than a less centered man, was president of the United States during the Cuban missile crisis, the key historical instance of Cold War danger.

Related to the deeply arguable contentions about the "good" purposes nuclear weapons have served is the implicit idea that their history somehow has completed chapters, the now concluded Cold War period being one of them. This is wrong. It is plain that interest in the acquisition of nuclear weapons is growing in various quarters, and the cases of recent proliferation demonstrate that the story of nuclear weapons in human history is far from over.

A more central reality is that this history has continuity. There is an indelible relationship between the continued possession of nuclear weapons by the established nuclear-weapon states and the will by others to acquire them. Nuclear weapons create precisely the danger that it is claimed justifies their existence.

If the history of nuclear weapons is to be brought to an end, it must start with those who possess them to decide to make it so. They have a clear choice: to build a world free from the greatest of all threats to life, or to prepare for the next stage of nuclear bondage and terrorism.

3

The Non-Proliferation Regime

If I were asked to identify the central truth or lesson I have learned from almost thirty years of working as a professional diplomat and negotiator in the X-file-like world of nuclear weapons, it is this: Nothing grabs the attention, fires up the ruthless determination of the owners of nuclear weapons more sharply than the prospect that they might have to give up those weapons or admit others to their private club.

Six years ago, in the spring of 1995, at UN headquarters in New York, the nuclear-weapon states faced just such horrors. The first twenty-five years of the Nuclear Non-Proliferation Treaty (NPT) had run out. It had to be extended by agreement among *all* of its members, not just the nuclear-weapon states, or it would lapse.

The nuclear-weapon states wanted indefinite, unconditional extension. The treaty had served the purpose of maintaining their exclusive club brilliantly in spite of the fact that they had never kept their side of the treaty bargain to continually reduce their own weapons and end nuclear testing. They had enjoyed a virtually free ride and wanted it to continue.

Their problem was that they needed the agreement of those they had steadfastly rejected or ignored—the non-nuclear-weapon states. Repeated attempts had been made during the preceding ten years to bring the nuclear-weapon states into line with their own undertakings, but those efforts, at the last moment, had wilted under extreme pressure from the nuclear-weapon states or had been bought off. In 1995, the signs were that such tactics would not work again.

The anxiety among the nuclear-weapon states was electric. They sent their heavy hitters to New York, and they brought in truckloads of technology with which to "monitor" the conversations and messages of key delegates.

One of the ways I came to know that I was considered to be one of the chosen was the frequency, and indeed on occasion bluntness, with which representatives of Western nuclear-weapon states—that is, "friends"—would indicate that they knew exactly what I had been saying to others, especially our "enemies."

An inverted snobbery system arose, reminiscent of the time twenty years earlier when a beleaguered President Richard Nixon's hate list was leaked to the press. Some distinguished citizens had felt very hurt that they were not on it. At the NPT Review Conference, I encountered delegates who were disappointed that they had not had it intimated to them by the Americans, British, or French that it was known what the delegate had been saying and reporting back home.

Amusing though this might be, it was in fact a deadly serious time. The global regime to prevent the spread of nuclear weapons was in jeopardy. The nuclear-weapon states were stuck between the rock of wanting it preserved and the hard place of their own willful failures. Their initial answer to this conundrum was to behave as bullies. My direct observation of this period is the main reason for the answer I have just given to the question, What have you learned? Parodying Dr. Johnson's observation about how the gallows tend to concentrate a man's mind, so it is with the nuclear-weapon states and the prospect of nuclear arms control.

As will be seen later in this chapter, the bullying hit the wall; it did not work. So another solution had to be found. It took the form of a series of documents on nuclear disarmament and what could be simply described as a prescription for generally better behavior, in the future, by the nuclear-weapon states. As is customary in such large diplomatic meetings, these documents had a multiplicity of authors. The main conceptual outline of them, however, was drawn up by the delegation I headed.

Oddly, the stimulus to drawing up this outline arose from concerns Australian authorities had held about the role that Israel might play in conjunction with the conference. The question of Israel had always been inflammatory at the NPT review conferences. It is not a party to the NPT and is widely believed to possess nuclear weapons. Its own policy on that matter is one of ambiguity—neither confirm nor deny its weapons status.

In 1995, the Australian authorities had become convinced that a number of countries might make the nuclear weapons status of Israel a key issue on whether they would agree to an extension of the NPT. The view was formed that Israel's own behavior, with respect to the conference, would be a factor. It was clear that it would not join the treaty, but the situation would be aggravated if it were to adopt a derisory or arrogant attitude toward it.

Two months before the opening of the conference, Canberra asked me to visit Israel to seek its cooperation. I spent two days in Jerusalem in a series of talks at the Israeli foreign ministry. At the end, I obtained agreement that, in conjunction with the conference, Israel would issue a statement that it supported the objectives of the treaty. That statement was issued at the beginning of the NPT Review Conference.

It was during the long flight to Israel that I, along with one of my colleagues from Canberra, designed the concept of documents on future work under the NPT, separate from the extension decision, but to be adopted with it as a means of solving the overall 1995 extension problems.

We subsequently handed this package to the South African delegation in New York and asked them to promote it, if they agreed with the approach. We judged that their influence would be considerable because of their new post-apartheid and post-nuclear weapons status. South Africa agreed and then played a major role in the subsequent negotiations.

Having been the subject of some three weeks of intensive, line-by-line negotiation in a representative group of some twenty countries, including the five nuclear-weapon states, the possible final form of these documents was emerging, but the countries were by no means agreed. For that to be achieved, it was necessary for a smaller group to meet away from the UN basement which had become the oppressive home of the twenty delegations for countless hours.

At the request of others, that move, on the second to the last night of the conference, was to the dining room of my apartment at Beekman Place, the residence provided to me by the Australian government, as it had been provided to successive Australian ambassadors to the United Nations for almost forty years.

I invited sixteen key players: the five nuclear-weapon states, the leaders of the non-aligned movement, some Western non-nuclear-weapon states, and Iran. Dinner started late, well after 9 P.M., fueled by not excessive quantities of Australian wine. The table conversation moved slowly from the periphery of the issues to the core. It established, above all, that the moment was serious. The nuclear-weapon states would have to agree to the draft documents or the NPT would not be extended without a vote. If there was a vote, the extension would almost certainly go through, but the vote would be seriously divisive, the numbers would be poor. The practical fact was that the treaty would be wounded, possibly mortally, even though formally it would be alive—on life support.

We moved from the table into the sitting room where I had set out sixteen comfortable chairs and, of course, coffee. At about 2 A.M., agreement was reached. All would agree to the package of documents. All would implement them faithfully. We would all pass the word around next day, and twenty-four hours later, when the documents were printed, meet in a formal session of the whole conference to adopt them.

Naturally, there was a sense of relief, even a touch of achievement, but it would be deeply misleading to say that there was confidence, either at 2 A.M. or a day later in the UN General Assembly that the promises given by the nuclear-weapon states would be kept.

The NPT was extended indefinitely, without a vote and without formal conditions or reservation. Within a year, the program of improved work agreed to in the associated documents had commenced, and the negotiation of the text for a comprehensive nuclear test ban treaty was concluded. Things appeared to be changing.

But then the momentum stopped. Crisis returned five years later, at the 2000 NPT Review Conference, and perhaps predictably another desperate deal was done. Its substance, now only a year old, is already unraveling.

It would be fair comment to declare all of this a circus, in every sense of that fine Latin word: something that simply goes around and around, or a tragicomedy with glitzy performers, none quite real.

What has been and remains in play is raw power, massive and unequally distributed, the indelible, primary manifestation of which is the possession of nuclear weapons.

What is at stake is to reduce the possibility that those devastating weapons will be used by preventing their spread to a multiplicity of nations and by eventually eliminating them. One instrument alone has been created to do these jobs—the Nuclear Non-Proliferation Treaty. It is because of its critical role in the preservation of civilization that it is given a central place in this book.

The Charter of the United Nations, constructed half a century ago at the conclusion of World War II, provides the framework of contemporary international relations and, incidentally, the context for understanding the NPT. The intention of those who framed the UN Charter in 1945 was to establish a new and legal structure for all future international relations. Their intention has been repeatedly confirmed by the interpretation of the UN Charter as a constitutional document by both states and courts.

Accordingly, the UN Charter sets forth *both* the structure of international relations and the rules of conduct within the community of nations, including the primacy of the sovereign state; the right to self-determination of peoples; the non-use of force; the peaceful settlement of disputes; respect for international rule of law; the universality of human rights; and the right to self-defense.

These concepts existed before the UN Charter was written, but they had never before been so codified in a single document designed to have binding constitutional authority. All states that accede to the UN Charter are expected to observe the obligations UN membership establish and, of course, enjoy its protection and privileges.

The UN Charter, however, took no account of nuclear weapons. It did not because these weapons had come into existence just as the UN Charter was being negotiated in San Francisco. The motivating concern expressed in the Charter was "to save succeeding generations from the scourge of war, which twice in our lifetime has brought untold sorrow to mankind." The Charter only makes reference to arms control—"the regulation of armaments"—and calls for plans for such regulation to be drafted. Although this has not happened in the designated terms, the subsequent development of arms control treaties by states has largely been conducted under the aegis of the United Nations. The NPT is a case in point.

On January 24, 1946, the first resolution adopted by the newly created General Assembly of the United Nations was on the subject of nuclear disarmament.[1] It is more than interesting to reflect on what the UN Charter itself may have stated on nuclear weapons had it been written as little as five years later, when the nuclear arms race was evident, assuming that it would then have been possible to reach agreement on a Charter, as such.

Given the intent and provisions of the UN Charter, and given the assumption that it would "maintain international peace and security,"[2] it can be asserted that to be complete, the Charter should contain provisions relating to nuclear weapons. Their unique character and impact upon peace and security, and indeed human survival, would justify such an insertion. It is for this reason, but also because the process involved in amending the UN Charter is torturous, that the NPT should be seen as supplemental to what is plainly the constitutional document of contemporary international relations.

This is no inflated assertion, preferred only by those who, like me, place great importance on the control of nuclear weapons. It rests on a recognition of specific, basic facts: The NPT establishes a norm of international relations; it is a treaty adhered to by virtually all states; and it deals with a matter of utmost, existential importance. For these reasons, it needs to be seen as comparable in stature to the UN Charter.

If this reasoning is applied to the body of major treaties or agreements concluded since the end of World War II—the matters at issue are of utmost importance, a norm is established with respect to them, and they are virtually universally adhered to—then the principal elements of the post–World War II international architecture can be identified as the following: the UN Charter; the Universal Declaration on Human Rights;[3] the NPT; and possibly the Nuremberg Trial principle of individual responsibility for crimes against humanity.

The norm established in the NPT is that no state or person should possess nuclear weapons. This touches upon all of the other international norm-setting instruments described here, with their focus on peace, security, and the sanctity of human life. On the latter, it is relevant that the advisory opinion of the International Court of Justice, given in July 1996 in the Nuclear Weapons Case, held that the use of nuclear weapons would violate humanitarian law.[4] The court had been asked by the UN General Assembly to provide an advisory opinion on "the legality of the threat or use of nuclear weapons."[5]

The need for a treaty on non-proliferation of nuclear weapons began to take form as Cold War tensions mounted in the late 1950s and the nuclear arms race entered its second decade. Growing concerns within the international community over the spread of nuclear weapons prompted the UN General Assembly, at the initiative of then Irish Foreign Minister Frank Aiken, to adopt a resolution, on November 20, 1959, on the feasibility of an international agreement on the non-proliferation of nuclear weapons.[6] Two years later, on December 4, 1961, another Irish draft resolution emphasizing the necessity of an international non-proliferation agreement was unanimously adopted by the UN General Assembly.[7]

A little more than a year later, and only five months after the Cuban missile crisis, President John F. Kennedy made remarks that subsequently have been widely regarded as having given crucial impetus to the development of the non-proliferation regime:

> With all of the history of war, and the human race's history unfortunately has been a good deal more war than peace, with nuclear weapons distributed all through the world, and available, and the strong reluctance of any people to accept defeat, I see the possibility in the 1970s of the President of the United States having to face a world in which 15 or 20 or 25 nations may have these weapons. I regard that as the greatest possible danger and hazard.[8]

Action on an agreement began when the UN General Assembly adopted a resolution assigning a mandate to the Eighteen Nation Disarmament Commission in Geneva to negotiate the Treaty on the Non-Proliferation of Nuclear Weapons (NPT).[9] That negotiation began immediately in 1965 and concluded with the treaty being opened for signature by states on July 1, 1968. The NPT has now been signed and ratified by 187 states. With the exception of the UN Charter, which has 189 adherents, the NPT is the largest multilateral treaty on record.

The NPT is rooted in reality. It begins by accepting, as a matter of fact, that there are two groups of states—those that have nuclear weapons and those that do not. The NPT specifically defines a nuclear-weapon state as one that had manufactured and exploded a nuclear weapon or other nuclear explosive device prior to January 1, 1967. The category of non-nuclear-weapon states included all others. The treaty stipulates that nu-clear-weapon states must

> undertake not to transfer to any recipient whatsoever nuclear weapons or other nuclear explosive devices or control over such weapons or explosive devices directly, or indirectly; and not in any way to assist, encourage, or induce any non-nuclear-weapon State to manufacture or otherwise acquire nuclear weapons or other nuclear explosive devices, or control over such weapons or explosive devices.[10]

This article of the treaty encapsulates the main contribution nuclear-weapon states are expected to make to non-prolifera-tion, that is, preventing the emergence of new nuclear-weapon states. It is an economical provision, but it is complete and un-qualified.

The non-nuclear-weapon states, for their part, are required by the treaty to

> undertake not to receive the transfer from any transferor what-soever of nuclear weapons or other nuclear explosive devices or of control over such weapons or explosive devices directly, or in-directly; not to manufacture or otherwise acquire nuclear weapons or other nuclear explosive devices; and not to seek or receive any assistance in the manufacture of nuclear weapons or other nuclear explosive devices.[11]

This is the symmetrical obligation to the first obligation, and like the first, it is complete and unqualified. These two obligations are designed to constitute the conditions for the non-proliferation of nuclear weapons among all states.

The NPT, however, is not intended to be only a mechanism for maintaining the status quo with respect to nuclear-weapon haves and have-nots. An additional obligation is embedded in the treaty, namely that states possessing nuclear weapons commit themselves to work toward nuclear disarmament. This undertaking assigns to the NPT a character that extends its original conception of preventing the further emergence of nuclear-weapon states. Article VI states:

Each of the Parties to the Treaty undertakes to pursue negotiations in good faith on effective measures relating to cessation of the nuclear arms race at an early date and to nuclear disarmament, and on a Treaty on general and complete disarmament under strict and effective international control.[12]

The text of Article VI meant that the NPT would become the first international agreement to enshrine the principle, as a norm of international life, that no state should have nuclear weapons. This is the irrefutable logic of an instrument that stipulates that all states not in possession of nuclear weapons should never change that circumstance and that those already possessing them should take action to divest themselves of those weapons.

The NPT both envisages and establishes the conditions for a world without nuclear weapons. It is, as a consequence, a paramount structure in the architecture of contemporary international relations.

The negotiation process for the NPT was difficult in the extreme, including many points of significant difference and argument. The treaty affirmed that nuclear weapons had already proliferated beyond those held by the original nuclear-weapon state, the United States and that the U.S. proposal for international control over nuclear weapons, the Baruch Plan of 1946, had failed and been replaced by the nuclear arms race.

Because the negotiation was conducted among unequal partners, the issue of equity was always centrally at stake. If the treaty merely prevented the emergence of further nuclear-weapon states, what could be said of the world that would remain? Would the world always be made up of nuclear haves and nuclear have-nots? The answer to these concerns was given in the restraints on nuclear disarmament contained in Article VI.

The question of what this legal restraint would mean to non-nuclear-weapon states—in terms of their access to the science and technology that are the by-products of nuclear weapons development—was also an important one. This matter had already been addressed in the 1954 negotiations on the Statute of the International Atomic Energy Agency (IAEA). In that case, a formulation was created in which the role of the IAEA would be to foster the exchange of scientific and technical information on the peaceful uses of atomic energy but to ensure that none of this information was used in such a way as "to further any military purpose."[13]

This formulation ensured that the negotiation on the Statute of the IAEA succeeded where the Baruch Plan had failed. That failure had been a product mainly of the Soviet Union's wish to become a nuclear-weapon state, but it also failed because the original proposal had dealt solely with control, leaving aside completely the question of access to nuclear science-derived technologies. The possibility that a consequence of control over nuclear weapons would be technological disadvantage for states that had agreed not to acquire them was a serious matter, especially for industrialized states. It was addressed in the Statute of the IAEA and, by extension, in the NPT.

The NPT describes, in brief terms, key actions that should be taken to implement the treaty undertakings and to support the goal of a world free of nuclear weapons. Chief among these are the entry by nuclear-weapon states into negotiations, "in good faith," toward the elimination of their weapons;[14] the negotiation of a treaty to ban all test explosions of nuclear weapons for all time;[15] and the entry by all non-nuclear-weapon states party to the NPT into a nuclear safeguards agreement with the IAEA to verify that they have adhered to their undertakings.[16]

The NPT is a peculiar treaty, to say the least, but two of its aspects are of critical importance. First, its creation rested on the bargain struck between nuclear-weapon states and non-nuclear-weapon states. Second, that bargain was struck only when it was agreed that the treaty would establish the norm that no state should have nuclear weapons. Equity among states was a central issue when the treaty was negotiated. It remains so today.

The NPT has grown in strength since its initial signature by 135 states. Over the thirty years since its entry into force, that number has grown to 187 states. Every sovereign independent state in the community of 191 nations has adhered to the treaty with the exception of four—Israel, India, Pakistan, and Cuba.

With respect to the non-nuclear-weapon states, the NPT has largely accomplished its objective. No such non-nuclear-weapon state party to the treaty has developed nuclear weapons. To assess the weight of this fact, it is important to recognize that at least 44 of those 187 states are viewed as capable of fabricating nuclear explosive devices were they to choose to do so.[17] Out of these potentially nuclear-capable states, there have been only three cases in which countries have violated their obligations to the NPT by seeking, on a clandestine basis, to develop nuclear weapons—Iran, Iraq, and North Korea. In each of these three cases, reports by the IAEA on their actions have varied in quality and detail. This has revealed weaknesses in the operation of the IAEA safeguards system in support of NPT.

The record of behavior under the NPT by nuclear-weapon states has been far less clear or satisfactory. For most of the treaty's life, the nuclear-weapon states either have not worked toward the elimination of their nuclear weapons, as had been pledged in the treaty or have made reductions only sporadically. There have been long periods of inaction, indeed extended periods, in which, contrary to their obligation, they have developed ever larger quantities and improved qualities of those weapons.

Since the 1980s, the disappointment of the international community with the failure of the nuclear-weapon states to keep their side of the bargain has emerged as a major threat to the NPT's continued viability. There has also been growing concern over the effectiveness of verification measures in the treaty, as underlined in the cases of Iran, Iraq, and North Korea.

Another major breakdown, up to the present time, has been the failure to bring into force a treaty banning all nuclear tests in all environments for all time, as called for in the NPT. Such a treaty was adopted by the UN General Assembly in 1996 and opened immediately for signature. The Comprehensive Test Ban Treaty (CTBT) has not yet been ratified for want of accession to, and ratification of, the treaty by the forty-four states specified in its text as being necessary for its entry into force.[18] A Comprehensive Nuclear Test Ban Organization was established to conduct the tasks of verifying and monitoring compliance with the terms of the treaty. It has not commenced all of its practical work because it must await the entry into force of the treaty.

The NPT originally stipulated that the treaty would remain in force for a period of twenty-five years. Furthermore, one of the treaty's provisions required a review conference on the operation of the treaty to be held every five years after its entry into force. There have been six review conferences to date.

At the NPT Review Conference in 1995, the original twenty-five years having passed, all parties to the treaty entered into negotiations to decide whether the NPT should continue in force indefinitely or be extended for an additional fixed period. As that conference approached, the Western nuclear-weapon states—the United States, the United Kingdom, and France—launched a major diplomatic effort to build support for their proposal to indefinitely extend the treaty. The campaign was marked by threats and bullying, addressed to both their Western partners and the majority non-aligned group of states. The principal instrument they brandished was a written pledge to be signed by delegation leaders at the conference to the effect that they would vote to extend the treaty indefinitely, if the matter came to a vote. Failure to sign the pledge, to climb on board the wagon, would bring unspecified harm.

Although Australia strongly supported indefinite extension, as the leader of the Australian delegation, I refused to sign the pledge, arguing that this tactic was abusive and would be counterproductive. I argued that the conference should debate the issues first, listen to the concerns of others, answer them, and then close political ranks.

I was threatened immediately by the leaders of the U.S. and U.K. delegations, and their governments took action at the highest levels in Canberra, Australia's capital, asking that I be pulled into line. The Australian foreign minister made clear that I was implementing Australian policy.

The pledge campaign was a disaster in terms of the number of signatures it attracted, but it did fuel the suspicions of a large number of non-aligned, non-nuclear-weapon states that the Western nuclear-weapon states wanted to freeze, in perpetuity, the situation of nuclear haves and have-nots. They feared, that if they agreed to an indefinite extension of the treaty, the five nuclear-weapon states would then feel released from the original bargain to eliminate their own nuclear weapons, while maintaining the strict obligation that no other state should acquire them.

As a consequence of this anxiety, various proposals for a limited extension of the treaty were advanced, including a plan to extend the NPT for another twenty-five years, or tying the extension to a specific time frame within which the nuclear-weapon states would be required to complete the elimination of their weapons; if they failed to do so, then the treaty would simply lapse.

A crisis developed, lasting for several weeks. There were resonances of the review conferences of 1980 and 1985. The former had resulted in no final document, signaling that the parties to the treaty did not agree that the treaty was operating as intended. The main reason then had been failure for any progress toward establishing the Comprehensive Test Ban Treaty. The blockage on that occasion had been led by the Mexican representative, Alfonso Garcia Robles, winner of the 1982 Nobel Peace Prize for his work on the Latin American Nuclear-Free Zone Treaty, the Treaty of Tlatelolco. Garcia Robles insisted that the treaty was a sham because the nuclear-weapon states failed to end nuclear testing and bring about significant reductions in their weapons holdings.

A similar situation had developed in 1985, again because of the continuing failure of the nuclear-weapon states to fulfill their treaty obligations and again, in some measure, as a consequence of Garcia Robles's stance. However, that conference was overshadowed more ominously by the Iran-Iraq War, which was in the fifth of its eight years. On that occasion, as Australia's deputy delegation leader, I negotiated a compromise between Iran and Iraq, between two and four in the morning on the last day of the conference, which resulted in a final, agreed document that Garcia Robles and his group were prepared to accept, if disconsolately.

Relief at mitigating the greater evil of the impact of the vicious war between Iran and Iraq, which had seen "the war of the cities," missile attacks by both sides on principal population centers, and the use by Iraq of chemical weapons, had sidelined the substantive failures of the nuclear-weapon states under the NPT.

At the 1995 conference, to overcome the contention surrounding the indefinite extension of the NPT, a series of documents was proposed that provided for a strengthening of the review process originally created in the treaty, the establishment of principles and objectives for further nuclear disarmament, a comprehensive test ban treaty to be concluded by 1996, and the negotiation of a treaty on a cutoff of the production of fissile material for nuclear weapons. These were considered, for some two weeks also, without agreement. I recorded at the beginning of this chapter what took place in order to achieve the NPT's indefinite extension.

The following year, the UN Conference on Disarmament in Geneva reached an agreement on a draft CTBT. India, however, refused to allow the text to be transmitted to the UN General Assembly in New York for its adoption, because it resented being among the forty-four states required to accede to and ratify the treaty before it would enter into force. It argued that another formulation could have been found if more time for negotiation had been allowed. At the time, India stated that it did not object to the main terms of the treaty nor to the concept that there should be a CTBT. It objected strenuously to being among the forty-four named states.

There was widespread discontent with India's stance, and this provoked urgent, private consultations on whether some action might be taken to circumvent it. Canberra proposed and

Washington agreed that I, by then Australian ambassador to the United Nations, might devise a solution. Canberra's initial thinking was that we might accomplish this jointly, with a key non-aligned state. Mexico was chosen because of its stature in the non-aligned movement and its track record on the nuclear test ban issue.

I traveled immediately to Mexico City for talks with Foreign Minister Jose Angel Gurria Treviño. He said he supported the proposed action in principle, but decided that Mexico could not take a leading role because of its sensitivities to India, a major non-aligned state. Australia decided then to go it alone.

For the subsequent month in New York, I held a recurring round of meetings with every member state of the United Nations to discuss and seek support for a procedural device I designed that would allow an identical treaty to the one negotiated in Geneva to be put as a resolution to the UN General Assembly. I met with member states three times in their regional groups, totaling some sixty meetings, before I was satisfied that the proposal would win. The resolution was then put to a special meeting of the General Assembly. It was adopted by a vote of 158 to 3 on September 10, 1996. Three countries—India, Bhutan, and Libya—voted against the resolution.

Shortly afterward, on September 24, 1996, I stood just feet away from President Clinton as he entered the first of what would be signatures by seventy-one states on the day the CTBT was opened for signature. I reflected on how twelve years earlier, a year after I had been appointed Australia's first ambassador for disarmament, the Reagan administration had privately approached the prime minister of Australia and asked that I be removed because of my strong advocacy for the CTBT. The then director of the U.S. Arms Control and Disarmament Agency, Kenneth Adelman, nicknamed me "Red Richard" during that period. But then, he once revealed to me that he thought that the democratic choice by the Australian people to install a government based on the Australian Labor Party, a year earlier, meant that a communist government had come to power in Canberra. Applying that reasoning today would mean that U.K. Labor Prime Minister Tony Blair is also a communist.

I have never ceased to marvel at how even well-educated American conservatives seem unable or unwilling to distinguish between communism, socialism, and social democrats. But theirs seems to be a very black and white world, even when they consider electoral outcomes in other democracies.

For the record, Australian Prime Minister Bob Hawke rejected the Reagan administration's demand for my removal, and I remained ambassador for disarmament for another four years.

The CTBT now bears 161 signatures, but three years after it was signed by President Clinton on October 13, 1999, the U.S. Senate declined to ratify the treaty. This action was deplored around the world as a significant setback to nuclear arms control and to the NPT.

The U.S. Senate rejection of CTBT ensured that the 2000 NPT Review Conference would be highly contentious. Two other factors reinforced these circumstances in spite of the crucial promises that had been made: Virtually nothing had been done by the nuclear-weapon states in fulfillment of the disarmament undertakings given at the 1995 NPT Review and

Extension Conference; and the CTBT had not entered into force, as called for at that conference.

In the weeks immediately before the 2000 NPT Review Conference, an additional and disturbing factor was introduced. The United States announced its intention to pursue the development of national missile defense (NMD), increasing the probability that the United States would either amend or, if necessary, withdraw from the 1972 Anti-Ballistic Missile (ABM) Treaty. As the first week of the conference commenced, the United States embarked upon what can only be seen as an extraordinarily insensitive, if not maladroit, diplomatic move by publicly attempting to persuade the Russian foreign minister, Igor Ivanov, to look benignly upon the U.S. missile defense plan and possibly agree to amendment of the ABM Treaty. He was unimpressed.

In ways that were again chillingly reminiscent of crises experienced during earlier review conferences, the 2000 NPT Review Conference teetered on the brink of failure. There was credible corridor discussion of the possibility that a whole bloc of non-aligned states might decide to leave the treaty. In the closing hours of the conference, this development was averted through the negotiation of thirteen steps. These included, once again, the entry into force of CTBT and the negotiation of a treaty banning the production of fissile material for nuclear weapons; the entry into force of START II and the conclusion of START III; and the development of verification capabilities to ensure compliance with nuclear disarmament agreements.

The five recognized nuclear-weapon states, realizing that the NPT was under threat, issued a declaration in which they stated their unequivocal commitment to the ultimate goal of a complete elimination of nuclear weapons. In that declaration, they seemed to go further than the terms of Article VI of the NPT, which does not use the word "elimination" as they now did. Their unqualified commitment to the elimination of nuclear weapons was seen as an advance.

Given the NPT's checkered history, this commitment by the nuclear-weapon states bears careful analysis. The May 2000 declaration of the nuclear-weapon states, stating that they were "unequivocally committed to fulfilling all their obligations under the Treaty," sat in stark contrast to their behavior.[19] On repeated occasions, when it seemed that the NPT might collapse because the five nuclear-weapon states failed to keep their part of the bargain, they managed to avert that event by reaffirming their commitment to nuclear disarmament. Up to the present, the treaty partners have been prepared to accept their statement.

Regardless of whether the nuclear-weapon states were sincere in that latest commitment to the "elimination" of nuclear weapons, it remains clear that they do not want those weapons to proliferate. This is the circle that they always tried to make square—preserving their own weapons in contradiction of the NPT bargain, while reinforcing the restraints the NPT places upon others.

That this choreography is losing its bounce is now plain for all to see. Two key developments signal the unraveling of the NPT compact: the recent emergence of India and Pakistan as nuclear-weapon states, quietly applauded by many non-aligned countries, and Israel's continued maintenance of a nuclear capability, which the United States has practically condoned. Add to this: cheating from within the NPT regime by Iran, Iraq, and North Korea in addition to the widely held expectation that other rogue states will emerge, and that a nuclear weapons capability might find its way into the hands of non-state or terrorist groups.

The future existence of the NPT and the aim of preventing proliferation hinges upon the conduct of nuclear-weapon states. But, in considerable measure, it also hinges on the degree of confidence invested by the NPT states in the effectiveness of the mechanisms designed to inhibit clandestine attempts to acquire nuclear weapons. Without this confidence, continued international commitment to non-proliferation is unsustainable.

The world is at a critical juncture regarding the future path of the non-proliferation regime. Weaknesses inherent in the International Atomic Energy Agency (IAEA) safeguards system have served to undermine the future viability of the treaty. If peaceful nuclear cooperation between states and the ability of the NPT to detect undeclared nuclear activities are to be enhanced, it is essential that the operation of the IAEA safeguards system be greatly strengthened. It is a matter of urgency.

Any examination of this means of verification, if it is to be accurate, must begin by recognizing the current inherent limitations of the IAEA safeguards system and the narrow scope of its mandate. The IAEA system involves inspections of the relevant activities of all treaty partners, the stated purpose of which is to detect the diversion of peaceful nuclear activities to any military activity. But this mission does not involve preventing such a diversion. It simply provides a means by which the occurrence, or apparent occurrence of it, is reported publicly. The philosophy involved here is somewhat akin to that of deterrence—if a state knows that its illegal activities will come to attention, that should serve to deter them from conducting such activities.

This thinking has two clear features. The first is the notion that the safeguards system will be effective and accurate enough to detect any diversionary activity. In large measure, this proposition has proven valid, especially when the relevant industrial and scientific infrastructure of an inspected state is relatively visible. But when a state has decided to embark upon clandestine fabrication of a nuclear explosive capability, essentially a criminal activity, it will seek to hide it. Given the nature and size of militarily relevant nuclear activities, this subterfuge is not easy to accomplish, but it can be pursued with some degree of effectiveness, as has been demonstrated by actual instances.

The second aspect of the deterrent effect of verification also relies upon the effectiveness of the means of verification for its validity; that is, the higher the possibility the clandestine activity will be detected, the greater its possible deterrent effect. Much more important however, is the question of whether a state determined to cheat has reason to think anything adverse will happen to it if its criminal activity is identified. If the cheating state is able to calculate that no reliable means exist to enforce its non-proliferation obligations, that detection of its activities will bring no remedy or punishment, then the deterrent effect at least wanes considerably, or even disappears entirely.

Another potential inhibitor of clandestine nuclear weapons development is action by states in possession of relevant technology and materials to prevent the transfer of those resources to states inclined toward cheating. Today, there are several multilateral arrangements that seek to control the trade and possession of nuclear weapon–related resources that could be used for military purposes.[20] These arrangements are based on the recognition that the control of transfers of relevant materials and dual-use equipment, which can be used for both peaceful and military purposes, is an integral and vital component a robust NPT.

Effective control over the transfer of nuclear material and technology is possibly the major weapon to be deployed against clandestine nuclear weapons development. The two fundamental necessities for such development are the scientific and technical knowledge involved in the fabrication of a nuclear explosive device and the availability of the special fissionable materials that will form the core of any such device.

Although both of the essential requirements for the fabrication of nuclear weapons exist in virtually all potential proliferating states, it is more often the case that they are not available in adequate measure. Major barriers can be placed in the way of any state seeking to enter into a clandestine weapons development program. If the states possessing the relevant resources either refuse to make them available, or if the attempts by a cheating state to acquire the relevant materials and technology are made public, the likelihood of nuclear weapons proliferation is vastly reduced. It is for this reason that a major aspect of the obligations of nuclear-weapon states, established in the NPT, is that they must never transfer to a non-nuclear weapon state any of the relevant technologies or materials. Obviously, the same is true with respect to the transfer of any fully fabricated nuclear explosive device, which is starkly prohibited.

Strengthening the NPT's effectiveness, especially with respect to rogue states, requires action on two fronts: improving the system for verifying state behavior under treaty obligations, and strengthening the international controls on trade in relevant technology and materials. Both of these objectives are achievable and should yield considerable benefits in terms of strengthening the NPT regime. What is required for such action is political resolve and determination on the part of major nuclear-weapon and industrial states.

The proliferation clock is ticking again, indeed at a quickening pace. All concerned states must face this reality, but that is particularly true of those that hold the greatest responsibility—the nuclear-weapon states. The choice those states face is between strengthening measures against proliferation, on the one hand, or taking measures of counter-proliferation, that is, building new weapons—an arms race—on the other.

It is beyond doubt that the choices they make will determine whether President Kennedy's prediction of forty years ago will prove true. Failure to make the first of these choices and instead to prefer measures of counter-proliferation, would involve abandonment of the fundamental goals of non-proliferation and nuclear disarmament. The NPT would not survive such a choice, and that loss would be compounded by the likelihood that defensive counter-proliferation measures would themselves fail because they would inevitably ensure the growth of what they were seeking to defend against—the ever increasing development of nuclear weapons and their spread to a multiplicity of countries.

The only sure way for the nuclear-weapon states to prevent such a world from coming into existence is for them to begin working toward the preferred world. If they choose to take such action, they must begin by first looking at themselves.

Nuclear-weapon states must materialize the promise they made in the NPT and have repeated *seriatim* right down to May 2000. Only if they design and implement a program of progressive nuclear disarmament, including the associated agreements on nuclear testing and the cutoff of manufacturing of special fissionable material, will the nuclear proliferation regime be preserved.

The anxieties that nuclear-weapon states may have about their own security and defense can be dealt with by non-nuclear means and collective action. If they choose to, they can also build enforcement mechanisms and address the deepest anxiety felt by the overwhelming number of NPT states—that in the event treaty obligations are breached by a determined transgressor, there will be no enforcement of its obligations.

Some will argue that such an approach to enforcement is too grand, too large, too hard to build and that the horse will already have bolted over the hill by the time such a system is ready. What is involved is complex, but it is wrong to assert that it cannot be done, that the task is an impossible one. It can be done if there is a will to do it. Even an indication of movement in that direction, such as the entry into negotiation by major states on the establishment of a reliable means of enforcement, would send a clear signal around the world that at last the undertakings of the NPT were going to be protected. This would have an immediate, widespread, and positive effect.

It would be wrong to fail to recognize the depth of cynicism that exists among non-nuclear-weapon states about the game nuclear-weapon states have played under the NPT. There is a limit to the patience with that game. When skepticism is expressed within nuclear-weapon states about the viability or the verifiability of the NPT, they typically fail to recognize how strongly committed a host of states are to the NPT objective and how much bitter disappointment they have had to swallow with respect to the behavior of their nuclear-weapon state partners. The nuclear-weapon states have also failed to recognize how much goodwill could be generated among their treaty partners were they to carry out their responsibilities earnestly and vigorously rather than continuing the brinkmanship they have played with the NPT through the years.

If the nuclear-weapon states want to preserve the objective of nuclear non-proliferation, they must start by paying the stated, agreed-to price for that objective—measures of self-denial. No one expects or requires that those measures should be so harsh as to jeopardize their security. But as important, virtually no one accepts the iniquitous proposition that the security of the nuclear-weapon states uniquely justifies their continued maintenance of nuclear weapons.

The alternative course of action, the adoption of measures of counter-proliferation, while touted as tough and acknowledged to be extraordinarily costly, are actually the easy way out. But worse than that, they are illusory. The very idea that the United States could obtain acceptance from China, for example, of the proposition that the new defensive systems it might develop are not directed at China, but at rogue states like Iraq, is extreme folly. It is also incredible; the test would be to put the shoe on the other foot.

What would be the position of the United States if China, as a nuclear-weapon state, were to proceed to develop new kinds and qualities of long-range nuclear weapons capable of harming the United States or weapons claimed to be merely defensive, yet insist that these were not directed at the United States? The howl of skepticism in Washington would be heard around the world.

The NPT contains a norm that is sound in terms of both international security and morality. Its latter aspect asserts that it is simply beyond any concept of civilization to maintain the security of any state or person on the basis of the threat of mass destruction of others. It is inevitable that as long as the threat exists, others will seek to defend against it by measures of a similar kind. The consequence of such action and reaction is an endless spiral of proliferation—precisely the spiral that the NPT correctly identifies as unacceptable.

What *is* required in all nuclear-weapon states from policymakers and from those who would seek political office is the courage to take the tough decisions to prevent the spread of nuclear weapons.

The only sure means by which that can be achieved is to take concerted action toward the elimination of all nuclear weapons and to ensure that they are never again created, through the maintenance of political and military enforcement arrangements designed to ensure that the law is obeyed.

4

Proliferation Today

Former Russian President Boris Yeltsin acquired a reputation for idiosyncratic behavior, not without justification or, indeed, extraordinary efforts by him. Yet, toward the end of his presidency, on December 10, 1999, he spoke of dark things with riveting clarity. Angered by U.S. statements on Russian actions in Chechnya, he warned the United States to remember that Russia still "possesses a complete arsenal of nuclear weapons."[1]

What was Yeltsin saying—that Russia would threaten the United States with nuclear weapons if it persisted in "interfering" in what he considered to be an internal Russian matter? Although hard to believe, it is not *absolutely* impossible. The United States, after all, would not tolerate any external interference in the United States in the extraordinarily unlikely event that such might occur.

Far more likely is that he was venting a much more complex anger and frustration—the loss by Russia of its status as a co-equal superpower. He was saying, in a rather American way, "Don't mess with us!"

What was all too real was the reason he gave for his warning—Russia's continued possession of nuclear weapons. In this respect, he was speaking the truth.

No matter what losses Russia has experienced since the collapse of the Soviet Union, and they been many, deep, and hurtful, none has compared to its loss of global status. The one hedge it believes it has against further pain and loss is its nuclear weapons, and Yeltsin, no matter what else he did or did not understand, understood this. He understood raw power in a way his somewhat hapless predecessor, Mikhail Gorbachev, did not. His successor, Vladimir Putin, understands power, above all else.

Yeltsin's statement had obviously unintended consequences. It underscored two key facts: First, the central issue in global survival remains that of coming to terms with nuclear weapons; second, any action toward that end must have at its core the forging of an understanding with the other power possessing a major arsenal of nuclear weapons—Russia.

Today's Russian president, dedicated as he is to restoring Russia's global prestige, second only to his maintaining power within Russia, will be a far more resolute and durable leader than Boris Yeltsin.

The United States will have to deal with Putin's Russia for a considerable time, and he has already served unambiguous notice that a key part of the relationship will be the strategic one, of which nuclear weapons form the core. The foundation of the management of that core has been a structure of nuclear arms control treaties. It needs to be reshaped to contemporary, post–Cold War circumstances, not torn down, as some members of the Bush administration are proposing.

The established structure of nuclear arms control treaties and agreements has been divided into two categories. The first is directed at containing and then reversing the vertical proliferation of nuclear weapons, that is, the increasing qualities and quantities of the weapons held by nuclear-weapon states. The second is aimed at preventing horizontal proliferation, or the spread of nuclear weapons to other states.

Although these two categories can be identified separately, they are connected systemically because of the provisions of the Nuclear Non-Proliferation Treaty (NPT). Equally important is their clear political connection: Success or failure in the first category influences progress in the other.

Reversal of past vertical proliferation needs to be reinvigorated. Nothing has occurred to reduce U.S. and Russian holdings of strategic nuclear weapons for a decade. Interestingly, this is the period since the declared end of the Cold War. It was widely anticipated that the end of that conflict would lead to significant further reductions in nuclear weapons. This has not occurred.

It is inconceivable that work on reductions of nuclear weapons can be reinvigorated if the United States does not make such action a fundamental part of its political relations with other nuclear-weapon states. U.S. leadership is the necessary condition for further reductions. If any other nuclear-weapon state were to initiate this action, whether unilaterally or through multilateral negotiations to that end, nothing of substance would transpire, absent the willingness of the United States to participate fully. It is very doubtful that the United States would be prepared to take any meaningful part in such a process unless it was initiated and led by the United States. In this context, it should be recognized, however, that it would be a mistake for the United States to identify its potential leadership with the notion of dominating or dictating the terms of the process.

True leadership, in this context, would be expressed much more effectively by way of an invitation issued by the president of the United States. That first invitation should be to Russia to join with the United States, as a co-equal nuclear-weapon state, in further reductions of strategic nuclear weapons. After initiating the joint process of reductions, they could seek to include all other nuclear-weapon states.

In addition to the deeply important intrinsic benefits the United States and all others would gain from reductions in strategic nuclear weapons and the restoration of momentum to nuclear disarmament, a U.S. initiative directed at the Russians would produce other important collateral benefits. Chief among these would be much needed improvement in U.S. relations with Russia, which is a country weakened in many ways, but still a dangerously armed nuclear-weapon state.

Following the Yeltsin event in late 1999, and since Vladimir Putin's election to the Russian presidency, Russia's military leadership has been enhancing the country's reliance on nuclear weapons for national defense, partly in reaction to the increasingly parlous state of its conventional armed forces. In January 2000, President Putin signed a new national security doctrine that drops its no-first-use of nuclear weapons pledge and considerably broadens the circumstances under which Russia would employ its nuclear weapons.[2]

As already indicated, among the many losses Russia believes it has suffered as a consequence of the collapse of the Soviet Union and the end of the Cold War, none has bitten more deeply than its loss of global status and influence and its standing as a co-equal competitor with the United States. Although nothing has been lost to the West, or to the states previously subjugated by the Soviet Union as a consequence of its collapse, the profound change in Russia's international status has been felt deeply and resentfully inside Russia. This is the stuff of serious political trouble.

The Putin government is now clearly embarking on a range of actions designed to reverse those circumstances. They have taken a form redolent of the Cold War period. Putin's visits to China, Cuba, North Korea, and Vietnam, and the signature, in July 2001, of a Russia-China cooperation agreement have signaled a policy of developing close relationships with states whose main characteristic is that they have, in various degrees, troubled relationships with the United States. He has sought to establish special relationships within the NATO area, specifically with Germany and to some extent with France, drawing as much as possible on their known reservations about the uses of the unprecedented power of the United States.

Russia's patronage of Iraq and Saddam Hussein, possibly including clandestine support to his weapons programs, has been an unalloyed throwback to Cold War client statism. Russia's support of Iran and its weapons programs has also been a source of deep concern. These developments, of which it can be expected there will be more, have led to justified speculation in the United States that Russia would prefer a world closer to that of the Cold War period than the present one. This is possible hyperbole, however, because there is little reason to think Russia would prosper under Cold War II. More relevant is the need for Russia's economy to be modernized and to be made more transparent and less subject to domination by its extralegal operators. This would not be achieved by a return to a period of great hostility. Western capital and technology for Russia would dry up. Nevertheless, there is a deep nostalgia in Russia for the sense of national greatness it enjoyed during the Cold War period.

The source of greatest danger posed by Russia remains its nuclear weapons. The need to address this is beyond doubt, and since the end of the Cold War, the United States has actively done so in a variety of fields, including nuclear weapons safety at considerable financial cost.

The danger posed by Russia is not just that its state-controlled nuclear weapons remain targeted on the United States, or that the Russian government may be prepared to share its nuclear technology, at least in part, with states such as Iraq and Iran. The possible loss of that control, leading to leakage of Russian nuclear materials to others through the action of Russian criminal groups—the problem sometimes referred to as "loose nukes"—presents an equal threat.

Russia's nuclear weapons systems are degrading, and the government lacks the resources to correct the problem. Some assess that this is the motivation for the current Russian offer to the United States to reduce strategic systems to 1,500 on each side. Whether that is true or not, it is disturbing that a solution to the resource problem might be sought by Russia selling nuclear weapons or related materials to Iraq or other customers who are willing and able to pay breathtaking sums for such goods.

Russia's stocks of weapons-grade fissile material, the only component of a nuclear weapon that Iraq has previously lacked, are vastly in excess of its own requirements. Just how much of this material Russia possesses is not known precisely, and the security under which these stocks are kept has been observed to be ludicrously deficient. These circumstances are deeply alarming and lead many to believe that such material has already been stolen in Russia and shipped to Iraq, as reported by Iraqi defectors.

A U.S. invitation to Russia to join in a campaign to reduce nuclear weapons would extend the means of reducing a major threat and offer Russia a return to co-equal status on the key issue in the management of global security. It should be irresistible to Russia. If Russia were to reject such an approach, then we would all have learned something about the new Russia that we needed to know sooner rather than later.

It would need to be made clear to Russia that its restored status would bring commensurate responsibilities. It would be unthinkable for Russia to continue its patronage of Iraq or its exports to Iran, and it would have to bring its own nuclear inventory under immediate and effective control.

Obviously, Russia would bring its own set of a priori requirements of the United States before it would participate in any joint effort. The inevitable one would concern a U.S. decision to construct a ballistic missile defense system.

The United States would be justified in remaining firm on its right to consider such a defense. It has already discussed its plans with the Russians and could continue to do so.

Any suggestion by either the United States or Russia that reductions in their strategic nuclear weapons systems should be tied to agreement or postponement of U.S. ballistic missile defense plans would ignore the intrinsic necessity and benefits of such reductions. It is self-evident that a linkage between the two areas—nuclear weapons reductions and missile defense—would be tempting as a negotiating tactic, but to proceed in that way would bring about a failure with potentially devastating consequences—the unilateral erection of an unreliable defense shield and a resumed nuclear arms race.

The Bush administration is in the process of developing and articulating the details of its policies across the board. Clear and specific policies are needed in the linked areas of nuclear disarmament and the management of stable relations with Russia.

Strong action could likewise be taken with respect to horizontal proliferation, provided that the nuclear-weapon states take serious action on their own stockpiles. Major aspects of such action would include strengthening the NPT verification system, establishing a reliable means of enforcement for non-proliferation undertakings, and initiating political steps to address the security concerns that motivate states like India and Pakistan to proliferate and other states to consider following them.

The question of why states consider acquiring nuclear weapons deserves continuing study. The publicly stated reason typically given by these states—to provide for their national defense—is simply not credible. It is incomplete.

States also consider acquiring nuclear weapons for reasons not related to their own defense or to rational political problems. Too many states believe that the possession of nuclear weapons lends prestige or empowers the state in ways that, while not always rational, are often considered highly desirable. There are cases in which the acquisition of nuclear weapons serves imperialist or hegemonic purposes.

Iraq's nuclear weapons program is one example of this phenomenon. Saddam Hussein established a clandestine program in the mid-1970s with the objective of indigenously producing an arsenal of nuclear weapons. But before Iraq could bring its Osirak nuclear reactor into operation, sixteen Israeli warplanes bombed the site on June 7, 1981. In the mid-1980s, Saddam reestablished his nuclear weapons program, intensifying and expanding it to produce a device as quickly as possible. This was in anticipation of Iraq's August 1990 invasion of Kuwait. Saddam ordered a crash program to have a nuclear weapon ready by April 1991. Although technical problems would have certainly delayed that deadline, it was only the international coalition bombing in January 1991 that prevented Iraq from assembling the uranium, materials, and technology to produce Saddam's nuclear weapon. Defector reports now indicate that Saddam may, in fact, have been able to assemble a somewhat crude atomic bomb and may have tested it underground in 1989, although the international seismological network has not verified such an event. Such reports also indicate that Iraq has resumed work on nuclear weapons following the ejection of the UN Special Commission (UNSCOM) inspectors in 1998.

Unless political and diplomatic action is taken to address the regional concerns that motivate nuclear weapons acquisition decisions, it is extremely doubtful that those decisions would not be taken, or that the states concerned would agree to replace acquisition decisions with arms control arrangements.

The acquisition of nuclear explosive capability by India and Pakistan, far from serving their national defense needs, has actually placed them in the deepest jeopardy they have faced since their region was partitioned. A miscalculation by one state or the other could easily occur in the intractable conflict over Kashmir, especially when neither side has the kind of command and control mechanisms maintained by the United States and Russia.

Israel's maintenance of nuclear weapons capability likewise may satisfy national psychological needs deriving from the now mythologized status of events at Masada some 2000 years ago, or from the hideous experience of the Holocaust. Nuclear weapons are perceived by Israeli leaders as insurance for their nation's existence without depending upon any outside support. In any case, Israel's nuclear arsenal—estimated to hold between 100 and 200 weapons—cannot be considered anything other than weapons of last resort. They would almost certainly be just that—the last action Israel would ever take as a state if it were to use those weapons.

Israel's acquisition of a nuclear weapons capability in the 1960s, with significant French assistance, was motivated substantially by the regional hostility with which that state has lived for more than half a century. It is that hostility that must be addressed. The fact that other states in the Middle East also possess weapons of mass destruction is a security issue that needs to be dealt with as part of an overall regional peace settlement. Israel can continue to rationalize its nuclear capability only as long as Egypt, Iran, Iraq, Libya, and Syria maintain their chemical weapons and, most certainly, Iran and Iraq insist on pursuing their nuclear weapons aspirations.

In cases where nuclear weapons acquisition decisions are taken for reasons of aggrandizement or imperialism, then clearly such acquisitions would deliver a new threat to neighboring states and possibly beyond. This would legitimize concerted action by the major powers to eliminate any weapons capability being constructed for such purposes.

It is important to underscore, again, that action by the major nuclear-weapon states to address these regional problems will not be effective unless they are themselves seen to be seriously committed to nuclear arms control. The major powers will also be required to stop aiding or facilitating the proliferation activities of their client states. It has already been noted that the hallmark of the Cold War was the nuclear arms race, but another was client statism, the motto of which could be said to have been "the enemy of my enemy is my friend." This overall mentality needs to change. It has led Russia, for example, to maintain a supportive relationship with Iraq when Iraq was clearly in violation of both its NPT obligations and the binding decisions of the Security Council. Moscow has continued to supply its clients with the technology and know-how needed to manufacture biological, chemical, and possibly nuclear weapons along with the ballistic missiles to deliver them. In his February 2001 testimony before the U.S. Senate Select Committee on Intelligence, CIA Director George J. Tenet affirmed that

> Moscow . . . may be resurrecting the Soviet-era zero-sum approach to foreign policy. . . . [It] continues to value arms and technology sales as a major source of funds. It increasingly is using them as a tool to improve ties to its regional partners China, India, and Iran. Moscow also sees these relationships as a way to limit U.S. influence globally.[3]

Threatening recalcitrant states with nuclear weapons does not deter them, and helping them to develop nuclear weapons capability is a flagrant violation of international law, as China has done with Pakistan. What would need to replace this Cold War–type constellation is an agreement between the United States and Russia, to which other nuclear states could be invited. Such an agreement would guarantee that effective action will always be taken to remedy circumstances when a state is building a WMD capability, contrary to agreed international norms. A commitment by the United States and Russia and other nuclear-weapon states to eliminate nuclear weapons would provide them with the political and moral authority necessary to successfully persuade others to forswear WMD options.

Perhaps the greatest contemporary threat to the integrity of the arms control regimes comes from within. The so-called "rogue states," are countries that profess to adhere to nonproliferation commitments while they, in fact, have decided to clandestinely manufacture or acquire nuclear weapons. This concept has been most vividly dramatized in recent years by three states party to the NPT—Iraq, Iran, and North Korea. At the very least, they evidently have embarked upon preliminary stages of nuclear weapons development. Their actions have been discovered partly through inspections conducted under the International Atomic Energy Agency (IAEA) and partly as a result of intelligence surveillance by individual states and defector reports.

In cases where such infractions or suspicions arise, the NPT calls for the IAEA Board of Governors to consider the case and, if it so decides, to refer its concerns to the United Nations Security Council. Such a referral carries the implication that the Security Council will decide upon the remedy required and its implementation.

In the case of Iran, no such referral to the Security Council has taken place. In the case of North Korea, such a referral did occur in 1993, but due to political machinations, chiefly China's refusal to allow a sanctions resolution or any other action to pass in the Security Council, no agreement for a remedy was reached. Instead, a number of states, led by the United States, were forced to establish a mechanism outside the United Nations system, the Korean Peninsula Energy Development Organization (KEDO), to carry out the agreement negotiated by the United States and North Korea in 1994. KEDO was to provide North Korea two proliferation-resistant light-water reactors and heavy fuel oil for heating and electricity in compensation for the dismantling of its nuclear reactors.

A unique course of action was taken with respect to Iraq, chiefly as a consequence of its invasion of Kuwait and the international military action, sanctioned by the Security Council, mounted to reverse that invasion. When that action was completed, the Security Council agreed to far-reaching arms control requirements with respect to Iraq's weapons of mass destruction capability, including their nuclear weapons program. It was this disarmament program that identified Iraq's crash program for the development of nuclear weapons. IAEA inspectors concluded that Iraq would have been in a position to detonate a nuclear explosive device within some six months, had the coalition bombing not forced Baghdad to abort its program. As discussed earlier, defector reports now claim that the program had in fact succeeded. In any case, there is evidence that Iraq is again working on nuclear weapons.

The major issues at stake in preventing the emergence of rogue states are the adequacy of mechanisms to verify treaty compliance, the behavior of states with respect to the transfer of relevant technology and materials, and above all, the availability of reliable means of enforcement of treaty obligations and the political will among the major powers to undertake such enforcement.

One of the larger sources of contemporary anxiety with respect to the proliferation of nuclear weapons—and indeed other weapons of mass destruction—is that they may find their way into the hands of non-state actors or terrorist groups. All of what has been presented here regarding the observation and verification of the activities of states within the NPT regime applies to non-state actors and terrorist groups.

The possibility that such groups may themselves seek to fabricate a nuclear explosive device is somewhat smaller than that of a state. Few, if any, terrorist groups are in a position to build the scientific and technical structures required to fabricate a nuclear explosive device. If they were to do so, it would be easily detected unless such activity was hidden within the activities of a supporting state. If that were the case, then all that has been argued with respect to the activities of that state would apply, by extension, to those of the terrorist group to which it was giving protection and assistance.

It is virtually certain that any acquisition by a terrorist group of nuclear explosive capability could be achieved only through the assistance of a state in possession of that capability—either given directly or provided by individuals within that state who have slipped out of its legal control. This latter possibility is of deep concern, particularly since the collapse of the Soviet Union brought with it the prospect that nuclear-weapon relevant materials, or indeed wholly fabricated nuclear weapons, may fall into the hands of criminal groups within Russia who may seek—for personal gain and possibly for ideological reasons—to make those materials or weapons available to a terrorist group outside its borders.

Although the doctrine of nuclear deterrence was principally aimed at the Soviet Union, the United States has expanded the concept to include other non-nuclear threats. For the past ten years, the United States has maintained a policy of "calculated ambiguity"—an implicit threat of nuclear retaliation in response to a chemical and biological weapons attack. This form of asymmetric deterrence was first employed by Secretary of State James Baker while negotiating with Iraqi Foreign Minister Tariq Aziz immediately prior to the onset of the 1991 Persian Gulf War. Secretary Baker made it clear to Aziz that Iraq's use of weapons of mass destruction would be met with devastating vengeance.[4]

However, the U.S. policy of asymmetric deterrence is a deeply dangerous concept. It contains two paramount flaws. First, a nuclear response to a non-nuclear attack would involve crossing the nuclear threshold. This event would immediately raise the possibility that another nuclear-weapon state might deploy its own arsenal either to assist the state targeted by a nuclear attack or to reassert a balance of power. In either case, a crossing of the nuclear threshold would forever open the possibility of first-use of nuclear weapons in a non-nuclear situation. It should be noted, in this context, that the United States and other declared nuclear-weapon states have formally given an assurance never to use nuclear weapons against a non-nuclear weapon state party to NPT. This assurance is widely considered to be an essential support to NPT and the notion of preserving the nuclear threshold.

The second problem derives from the possibility that the threat of nuclear retaliation against a non-nuclear weapon state may not work. For example, if a state preparing to use chemical weapons ignored its adversary's threat of nuclear retaliation, the nuclear-weapon state could feel obliged to make its threat real, if for no other reason than to punish the offending state for ignoring its warning. The bluff involved in the policy of "calculated ambiguity" would have been called, the offending action not deterred, but the nuclear-weapon state then would have been put in a position it would find completely unacceptable—the revelation that its nuclear threats were illusory—and to redress this would use nuclear weapons, when in fact it had never intended to. Leaders such as General Colin Powell and Secretary Baker have acknowledged that the United States was not prepared to use the nuclear option against Iraq during the Persian Gulf War.[5]

Another situation of asymmetric deterrence also compels attention. This is the threat of a nuclear response to deter a terrorist attack upon a nuclear-weapon state. It is conceivable that if a nuclear-weapon state were to become aware of an imminent terrorist attack, depending on the nature and scope of the planned attack, it might feel obliged to take preemptive action by threatening a nuclear attack on the terrorist organization's base and the weapons it proposed to use.

Although to many this might sound muscular and prudent or both, such a policy does not survive careful scrutiny. In the first instance, the probability that a politically and ideologically determined terrorist group—having decided to attack the armed forces, embassies, or domestic facilities of a nuclear-weapon state—would in fact be deterred from that course of action by the threat of nuclear weapons is almost negligible. It is doubtful that such a group would find the threat of massively disproportionate use of force credible. Moreover, the possibility that a nuclear-weapon state would deploy its arsenal against a non-state actor would further fuel the ideology that supported the terrorist group's intention in the first place. Terrorist groups have a basic interest in obliging a hated state to conform to the brutal image they hold of it.

Any discussion of asymmetrical deterrence, if it is to be complete, would also need to take deep note of the moral outrage that would clearly follow any action by a nuclear-weapon state, which would be seen as swatting a fly with a sledgehammer.

Effective action to deal with terrorist groups is one of the more vexing questions in both international life and law enforcement today. The foundation of action to prevent terrorist groups from acquiring and using weapons of mass destruction remains the prevention of the transfer of such materials by states that possess them. The construction of such controls requires urgent and extensive cooperation among states. In those instances where such transfers have occurred, the case for immediate action to prevent the use of such materials is beyond reproach. The idea that such action could be the subject of vetoes in the Security Council should not be acceptable. There is sufficient law in existence on terrorism and the right to self-defense to make such action legitimate.

If any central truth has been learned during this half century of nuclear weapons, it is surely that they are unusable. They have not been used since the first two occasions. This is not to say that a decision to use them will not be made and implemented. It asserts that although the decision to use nuclear weapons would be based on the apprehension of a threat that appeared to require such a remedy, and the use of nuclear weapons might eliminate that threat in the immediate future, what would follow from that decision would be a set of problems larger than those it was supposed to solve. There would be no remedy.

The problems emanating from the effects of a catastrophic exchange of nuclear weapons would include the unleashing of insufferable environment and biological damage. Where that use had been contained to only a region of the world, the crossing of the nuclear threshold would legitimize future use of nuclear weapons for so-called limited purposes. Such an event would signal destruction of basic notions of decent civilization as we know it.

These facts define the utility of nuclear weapons. That utility is solely restricted to the threat of their use, as distinct from their actual use, specifically in response to other nuclear weapons. Although this notion of nuclear deterrence has been operable for almost fifty years, it has never been stable. It instigated the nuclear arms race and underlies the ever-present and increasing possibility of horizontal proliferation.

Employing nuclear weapons for asymmetric deterrence is both not credible and deeply dangerous. It could lead to the unintended use of nuclear weapons.

The United States must take the lead in developing measures to combat contemporary pressures toward proliferation. Although there is an established body of U.S. policy in the field of nuclear weapons proliferation, it is composed of many separate and sometimes internally contradictory elements. The overall content and direction of this policy fail to address contemporary realities, and the policy does not meet the central requirement of leadership. There is an urgent need for the United States to articulate a single and comprehensive nuclear disarmament, arms control, and non-proliferation policy as a major part of its national foreign and security policy.

5

Nuclear Defense

On May 18, 1974, India conducted its first nuclear test explosion. It had used a Canadian-supplied nuclear power reactor to produce the core material for its bomb. Its action shocked the world. India, nevertheless, claimed its test had been for purely scientific purposes and that it remained committed to nuclear disarmament—for which it had made and continued to make far-reaching, global proposals for the subsequent twenty years.

India had refused to join the Nuclear Non-Proliferation Treaty, claiming that it constituted an unfair arrangement in favor of the nuclear-weapon states. Twenty years later, as already discussed, India attempted to block international agreement on the Comprehensive Nuclear Test Ban Treaty. When I tabled that treaty in the UN General Assembly in 1995, the speech of opposition to the treaty given by India's ambassador to the United Nations, Prakash Shah, mentioned almost in passing, after pages of criticism of the treaty text, that India reserved the right to conduct nuclear weapons tests in the future.

On May 11, 1998, this quiet warning in Shah's speech was made real. India conducted a series of three underground nuclear weapon test explosions. It went on to conduct two more tests on May 13. Pakistan followed suit, announcing on May 28, 1998, that it had successfully carried out five nuclear tests.

I was asked by various news media outlets in New York to comment, presumably because of my role on the test ban treaty, but also because I was then very visibly at work on the attempt to disarm Iraq.

I made three points. First, I said, if anyone is surprised by these developments, then all they are really saying is that they have not been listening. India, in particular, had made it clear that it would do this. Second, if one wants to look for a cause, start with the nuclear-weapon states. India and many others had begun to despair at the failure of those states to keep their nuclear disarmament promises. And finally, what we have to work for is the prevention of a nuclear arms race in South Asia, beginning by encouraging India and Pakistan not to weaponize their explosive devices, that is, load them onto missiles.

In the three years since the Indian and Pakistani tests, the fears expressed in my comment have been realized. India has plunged ahead with weaponization, and further development of a fully articulated nuclear weapons capability for its armed forces is under way. This has been against the background of continuing hostility between India and Pakistan over the disputed territory of Kashmir, a problem born of the partition of India fifty-four years ago. This, among other factors, has led many commentators to describe South Asia as the prime regional candidate for the use of nuclear weapons.

The situation is complicated deeply by the fact that China, in absolute violation of its obligations under the NPT, assisted Pakistan with its test explosions. And Russia is aligned with India.

The situation of India and Pakistan is extrasystemic to the NPT, but it has shaken the treaty to its foundations. It is a story, the end of which has not yet been told. It needs urgent, direct attention.

All political leaders, whether in democracies at one end of the spectrum or in thoroughly authoritarian systems at the other, assert that their highest duty to those who elected them, or to those whom they claim to represent, is to maintain the security of the nation. That security has a multiplicity of faces, ranging from the territorial, cultural, and religious to the economic domains. Above all, however, the security of the nation-state is asserted by a range of actions designed to maintain its integrity and its very existence. Little compares to the passions and political determination that the notion of national security arouses. It is typically portrayed as an issue of life and death.

The question of how to provide for national defense is, therefore, one to which political leaders give concentrated and sustained attention. Their assessments of threats to the nation and their consequent commitments of resources to its protection are paramount features of their decisionmaking. As those assessments change, so do commitments to military capability, reflected in both quantities and qualities of deployed military resources. This decisionmaking process is ongoing and dynamic, reflecting the state's reaction to perceived increases in the military capability of potential rivals, or as a consequence of decisions by political leaders to pursue their interests externally, such as providing assistance to allies or accomplishing plainly imperial, ideological, or revisionist aims.

There is also another dynamic at play, perhaps especially in Washington. It is one largely hidden from public view. This is the interaction between research and innovation in weapons technologies and the policy decisions involved in arming U.S. defense forces to address specific threats or to achieve identified security tasks. It is always the case that new weapons, as they become available, can have an impact on the policy process. But if they shape or even come to dominate it so that national security policy becomes driven by available weapons technology rather than the reverse, then a crucial shift in logic, and possibly in the correct order of things under the U.S. Constitution, will have occurred.

The government elected by the people, not the military leadership, has the responsibility for the provision of national security. This is epitomized by the fact that the U.S. president, not the chairman of the Joint Chiefs of Staff, is commander-in-chief. The president is responsible for identifying the national security interest, and it is the president's responsibility to propose to Congress a budget for national security and other national purposes. When the technical possibilities of conceivable weapons systems take on a life of their own, disconnected from the fundamental task of *political* decisionmaking, the prospect of bad policy decisions increases sharply. This possibility reaches its height in the field of weapons proliferation. Whenever a decision is made to deploy a new and presumably superior weapon, it must be expected that adversaries will respond in kind. Any deployment decision, if it is to be sound, must take into account this proliferation reality and weigh it in the balance. Such considerations are inherently *political,* not technical or even military. It may be decided that the national security interest points to a deployment decision rather than the opposite, but that decision must be taken by the political leadership elected by the people.

Every state possessing nuclear weapons has justified its decision to acquire that capability in terms of national defense. Both India and Pakistan claimed that the reason for their May 1998 nuclear tests was national defense. Prime Minister Atal Bihari Vajpayee announced before India's parliament, "We do not intend to use these weapons for aggression or for mounting threats against any country; these are weapons of self-defense, to ensure that India is not subjected to nuclear threats or coercion."[1] Pakistan's Prime Minister Muhammad Nawaz Sharif issued a similar statement: "Our decision to exercise the nuclear option has been taken in the interest of self-defense. These weapons are to deter aggression, whether nuclear or conventional."[2]

The core justification that these countries chose to defend against the use, or threatened use, of nuclear weapons has been other nuclear weapons. The notion that the use of nuclear weapons could be deterred by the threat of conventional force has no validity.

The basic feature of the nuclear deterrence doctrine is the acquisition and deployment of a nuclear weapons arsenal sufficiently robust to convince any nuclear adversary that, were it to launch a first nuclear strike, it could expect a devastating, and therefore unacceptable, nuclear retaliation. It is asserted that if this threat is credible, it will deter a first strike with nuclear weapons.

This logic has always led to expansion in the acquisition of nuclear weapons. If one country's deterrent force is to be credible at any given moment, it raises the possibility, in the mind of its adversary, that it could also serve as a winning first-strike capability. The reaction of that adversary therefore is to move, as quickly as possible, to enhance its own nuclear capability to deter such a first strike, that is, to exceed the nuclear power of its rival. This dynamism, which is potentially endless, drove the nuclear arms race.

The main historic illustration of this dynamic and its dangers, including possibly miscalculation and loss of control, is the Cuban missile crisis of 1962. Ordinary Americans became convinced that the United States and the Soviet Union were on the brink of mutual annihilation. They were right. The solution President Kennedy found was diplomatic and political. Had he not achieved that, deterrence would have failed.

The United States and the Soviet Union followed a pattern of spiraling nuclear weapons development throughout the Cold War. Both sides steadily increased the number and power of their strategic systems to create a seemingly invincible triad of ground, air, and sea-based nuclear forces. The two countries sought to secure their missiles—chiefly long-range intercontinental ballistic missiles (ICBMs)—by storing them in hardened, concrete-reinforced silos and placing them on moveable platforms—bombers and submarines—that could escape a surprise attack or evade detection.

The development of multiple, independently targetable reentry vehicles (MIRVs) in the 1960s and 1970s signaled a new level of potential destruction. This innovation took place as the United States and the Soviet Union were moving ahead with the development of anti-ballistic missile (ABM) programs, which could potentially intercept the enemy's offensive missiles and neutralize its deterrent, or first-strike, capability. MIRVs were designed to penetrate and overwhelm an ABM defense, enabling a single missile to deliver a multiplicity of individually targeted nuclear warheads.

Although the stated purpose of strategic nuclear weapons is to maintain stability through deterrence, they have been the key elements in an inherently dynamic and potentially unstable system. In fact, this potential instability became the central feature of deterrence, which was believed to be achieved through the threat of mutual assured destruction.

The capacity of the American and Russian nuclear arsenals has increased, over the years, to the point where the explosive power carried by a single nuclear submarine rivals the conventional explosive power used throughout the course of the Second World War. A Trident strategic ballistic missile submarine, for instance, carries twenty-four ICBMs, and the eight nuclear warheads on each of those ICBMs are independently targetable, can reach any city around the world, and have an explosive power several times greater than the atomic bomb dropped over Hiroshima.[3]

Further developments led to the acquisition of nuclear weapon systems for tactical use or use in a specific theater of war. Both sides deployed intermediate-range vehicles and missiles within the European theater and developed nuclear weapons for use in specific battlefield situations, including miniaturized warheads that could be targeted against conventional forces over very short ranges and launched from small mobile vehicles.

Strategies for the use of nuclear weapons on the battlefield or in regional theaters, while highlighting their potential use against other nuclear forces, have in fact come to be recognized as largely theoretical. A succession of military officers responsible for the command and control of the U.S. nuclear arsenal have indicated that there was almost no circumstance under which they would feel prepared to ask for presidential authorization to use those weapons.

When Secretary of Defense Dick Cheney asked General Colin Powell, then chairman of the Joint Chiefs of Staff, to draw up plans for the use of nuclear weapons against Iraq in preparation for the Persian Gulf War, General Powell responded, "You know we're not going to let that genie loose."[4] Since then, General Powell has openly questioned the value that states, particularly developing ones, could gain from acquiring a nuclear capability: "I think there is far less utility to these weapons than some Third World countries think there is. What they hope to do militarily with weapons of mass destruction I can increasingly do with conventional weapons, and far more effectively."[5]

There have been repeated attempts over the years to develop both doctrines and technologies to defend against the great danger posed by nuclear weapons. The argument for building a means of defense against nuclear attack has enormous political resonance, especially in popular democracies. Although most people in stable and prosperous democracies have, for all practical purposes, become largely inured to the continuing danger posed by nuclear weapons, they do recognize their extraordinary power. They are, therefore, open to the simple logic of defending their country against these terrible instruments rather than developing more of them or relying solely upon the notion of deterrence, particularly if they believe that their adversaries will not behave rationally, a belief that is justifiably held of rogue states and terrorist groups.

Several versions of ballistic missile defense have existed since the early 1960s, but it was President Ronald Reagan who had the greatest success in convincing the American public that it was preferable to pursue a policy of defense instead of relying forever on what he considered to be the repugnant notion of mutual assured destruction.

In March 1983, President Reagan proposed the concept of Strategic Defense Initiative (SDI)—a space-based missile defense system that would accompany reductions in nuclear weapons—by posing some seemingly sensible questions: "What if free people could live secure in the knowledge that their security did not rest upon the threat of instant U.S. retaliation to deter a Soviet attack, that we could intercept and destroy strategic ballistic missiles before they reached our own soil or that of our allies?"[6]

The current stated rationale for building a national missile defense (NMD) system in the United States, if it is taken at face value, gives greater attention to the perceptions of irrationality and unpredictability in international affairs as opposed to the earlier version's emphasis on neutralizing a massive nuclear attack from a peer competitor. Indeed, Iraq's behavior in the invasion of Kuwait and then during the Persian Gulf War served to reinforce American concerns about vulnerability.

After it became evident that U.S. Army Patriot missiles managed to intercept only some 40 percent of the eighty-eight Iraqi Scud missiles fired at coalition forces and at Israel, Saudi Arabia, and Bahrain, the United States decided to transform SDI into a system that could more accurately counter missile threats from rogue states.[7]

The main reason now being advanced for NMD is to defend the United States against the action of rogue states—specifically, Iran, Iraq, and North Korea. Although it is conceded that none of these countries presently has long-range ballistic missile capability, or nuclear warheads, NMD advocates contend that those states are in the process of acquiring these capabilities and could have them within the next five years. Explaining the shift away from SDI in 1993, Secretary of Defense Les Aspin commented: "Saddam Hussein and the Scud missiles showed us that we need a ballistic missile defense for our forces in the field. That threat is here and now. In the future, we may face hostile or irrational states that have both nuclear warheads and ballistic missile technology that could reach the United States."[8]

The public argumentation for NMD asserts that the development of a ballistic missile capability by rogue states cannot be prevented and that such states intend to break whatever treaty obligations they have entered into in order to develop weapon systems capable of harming the United States. Although there is some evidence for the first part of this assertion, there is little or none for the second.

The exaggerated assertion of threat to the United States by rogue and/or new nuclear-weapon states has become basic to the administration's justification for building a national missile defense system. Secretary of Defense Donald Rumsfeld has spoken of "a situation where there are any number of countries that are developing weapons of mass destruction and the ability to deliver them."[9] He carefully avoids providing specific details of this claim. If this claim is true, the details should be provided to the public and the world community.

Proponents of NMD also assert that existing treaty and other control mechanisms are unverifiable. This claim misleadingly confuses verification with enforcement. The fact is that the activities and intentions of such states can be verified to very high levels of accuracy, if sufficient effort by international and national agencies is employed to that end. What is more difficult, and less certain, is that international action to enforce WMD norms will be taken. Again, rogue states could be prevented from pursuing such action if the major powers determined that they were prepared to enter into enforcement action, both politically and militarily.

The rationale for NMD recognizes correctly that preventative action, or action to enforce treaty undertakings, is difficult. The sleight of hand that is performed in asserting that the difficult is impossible undermines any concerted effort to achieve what is avowedly difficult but not impossible.

The proposed NMD system of the United States contains at least three major difficulties: the vast technical problems yet to be solved, the high cost of constructing the shield, and the effects an implemented NMD would have on the postures of other nuclear-weapon states.

First, the possibility that a truly effective defensive shield can be constructed is small. An important distinction must be drawn between defense deployed against an adversary's missile in boost phase, that is, when it is slow and hot, and interception is made easier by heat sensors, and against an adversary's missile in space, when it is fast and cold, making interception far more difficult. Current U.S. research is apparently focused on the latter, implying that contrary to the rogue state rationale given for NMD, it is in fact motivated by a decision that the United States should achieve military dominance of space. If this is the case, it is beyond doubt that the U.S. entry into space as an environment for the conduct of war would cause a new arms race.

It is of central importance in this context to recognize the dangers involved in coming to rely upon a shield that is less than fully effective. The concept of NMD does not allow for a partial or second best solution. The difference between an utterly reliable shield and one that contains holes is a major, not a minor, issue. Security would not be provided if the proposed NMD were permeable, so any serious degree of reliance on such a shield would be a major folly in national security because it would be false security. The mounting technical problems associated with NMD—the failure of two out of four intercept test flights, the delayed development of a new booster rocket, and the system's inability to overcome simple countermeasures such as decoys—led President Clinton to leave the final authorization of NMD to his successor, President George W. Bush.

Second, the issue of cost is by no means a small one. Estimates for building NMD are unreliable, but all have one feature in common—the cost involved would be enormous. The United States will spend some $60 billion on the land-based

NMD plan through 2015. However, proposals for a comprehensive missile defense that includes land, sea, and space-based components would significantly increase the cost: $15 billion for the addition of a sea-based system, $27 billion for space-based lasers, and another $18 billion for space-based interceptors. Such an ambitious plan would require outlays totaling approximately $120 billion.[10] Given the extreme orders of magnitude involved, it is essential to ask whether the objectives at stake could not be achieved by less costly means.

Third, and perhaps most importantly, is the potential impact that NMD would have upon other nuclear-weapon states. The notion that the United States could develop its shield without incurring wider international security implications is typically advanced in static terms. The United States will build NMD, its proponents claim, strictly for national defense, so other countries have no reason to react in any negative way. The United States is effectively asking Russia and China, in particular, to accept that the American defensive shield is directed solely at the so-called rogue states; it would have no impact on the security interests or nuclear deterrence capabilities of the other nuclear-weapon states. This stance would lose credibility if or when it became clear to others that U.S. policy is aimed at what the relevant internal planning documents style as "full-spectrum dominance" of space. Consistent with the principle that when the rational explanations advanced for a policy or event lack credibility or make no good sense, then one should look for the real explanation, the view is growing that the real, unstated motive for NMD is, in fact, to achieve such U.S. dominance of space.

To ask others to make the static assumptions called for by the administration is to ask too much. No rational policy planner in Moscow or Beijing could accept such an assurance. Instead, they would feel obliged to calculate what impact the U.S. defensive shield, without an associated change in its nuclear weapons capability, would have on their ability to deter a U.S. nuclear attack. Any such calculation would inevitably result in the most pessimistic conclusions in Moscow and Beijing.

In response, both Russia and China would reinvigorate their own weapons programs and seek to develop weapons, including nuclear weapons capable of piercing America's shield. Thus, the main consequence of the U.S. decision to build NMD would be to trigger a new stage in the nuclear arms race and possibly an arms race in space.

In the specific case of Russia, the administration wishes at least to amend if not withdraw from the U.S.-Russia anti-ballistic missile treaty of 1972, because the treaty prohibits the deployments the United States plans to undertake. The argument that the administration has advanced against that treaty plumbs the depths of incredulity; it is asserted that it is a Cold War relic, that it represents "a policy of vulnerability," and that it is part of "a whole set of treaties and arrangements that are structured on hostility."[11] Expanding on his notion that there is no longer any hostility between the United States and Russia, Secretary Rumsfeld stated that "obviously you negotiate with an enemy,"[12] but as Russia, according to him, is no longer in that category, there is no need to negotiate with it on the ABM treaty, even though Russia says it attaches fundamental importance to the treaty.

I do not think there is any purpose in characterizing Russia as the *enemy* but find it virtually meaningless to declare a complete absence of "hostility" between the United States and Russia when each country has some 6,000 strategic nuclear weapons targeted at each other, on hair trigger alert. What Secretary Rumsfeld describes as the need for the establishment with Russia of "a new relationship with them and a new set of understandings,"[13] will do better if it is rooted in the true state of affairs.

There is yet another grave consequence of a U.S. decision to pursue NMD: the impact it would have on the arms control and non-proliferation regimes. Proceeding with NMD would represent a major contradiction to the commitment the United States has made to work toward the elimination of nuclear weapons. Instead, it would signal a determination to continue to rely on nuclear weapons into the indefinite future. This stance would be in direct contradiction to U.S. obligations under the NPT and the pledges it and the other nuclear-weapon states have made.

Beneath these very considerable difficulties raised by the NMD proposal lie a number of more fundamental questions. The first of these concerns the threat from rogue states, the postulation of which is the justification advanced for NMD. Briefly stated, rogue states are in the process of acquiring missiles capable of reaching the United States or U.S. military targets elsewhere. Such missiles are merely vehicles to deliver a warhead, and on that question, it is implied that the warheads to be delivered may be nuclear. Two negative developments are identified: one in the missile area, another in the proliferation of nuclear weapons.

It is established that Iran, Iraq, and North Korea are working on the acquisition of long-range missile capability. The outcome of their efforts—what they will acquire and when—varies in each case. What is clear is that they will acquire an incomparably smaller capability than that of the United States, and the date by which they will have any significant capability is some five years into the future. These facts are recognized by the proponents of NMD, but they contend that a defensive shield would itself take some years to build, so work must start *now*.

On the foreseen nuclear warheads, the prognosis is less clear. Of the three rogue states cited, each is suspected of working on acquiring nuclear explosive capability and, as in the case of Iraq, may already have done so. In each of these cases, such action would be a breach of their NPT obligations, and this should mean, under present arrangements, that their actions would be placed before the UN Security Council as constituting a "threat to international peace and security." The Security Council should then be urged to take remedial action. It is not suggested that this would yield a ready solution, given the track record of the Security Council on such issues.

What is suggested, however, is that up to the present, the failure of the United States to raise these matters at the Security Council is serious. It squanders a significant political opportunity to focus attention on outlaw behavior, which would bring the United States an opportunity to defend itself against charges of arrogant unilateralism should it decide to take action against a rogue state. And, President George W. Bush has said he would do exactly that if the United States finds Saddam developing weapons of mass destruction: "Our intention is to make sure that the world is as peaceful as possible. And we're going to watch very carefully as to whether or not he develops weapons of mass destruction. And if we catch him doing so, we'll take the appropriate action."[14]

It is dangerously unclear what President George W. Bush means by "catching" Saddam. Claims by the United States that it has made such a catch, absent the presence in Iraq of international inspectors, are likely to be met with skepticism, if it does not first refer its concerns and evidence to the Security Council. Knowledge of this fact and the wish to hide his weapons development work is precisely why Saddam Hussein has refused to accept international inspection for the past three years.

If it is granted that a threat of the kind currently identified is emerging, and this leaves aside the manifest and repeated instances of exaggeration of that threat by NMD promoters, some of whom speak of "massive" proliferation being underway, then the burning question that arises is how best to address, indeed redress, it.

Drawing on the core doctrine that has supported the development and deployment of nuclear weapons for almost half a century—deterrence—it is relevant to ask why it is being so lightly abandoned this time. Why, for instance, is the United States not content to make clear to the rogue states that any decision by them to develop a WMD threat would be met with an intolerable response? Such a threat could be expressed effectively with conventional weapons, given their power and precision, and could be exercised at an earlier, rather than later, stage of the rogue WMD development. Some critics of the basic and shifting rationales for NMD have asked, What happened to good old-fashioned deterrence? Dare it be asked whether deterrence is no longer reliable? Have its acolytes lost the faith?[15]

An accurate assessment of the nature of the rogue state threat would suggest that an attack from such a state would most likely be delivered through chemical or biological weapons, possibly a nuclear weapon, using far simpler and probably unidentifiable vehicles as far as their origin was concerned—a briefcase carried or a truck driven by a terrorist. To fire a missile at the United States would be to send a message with an unambiguous return address. Under present circumstances of U.S. weapons capability, conventional or nuclear, such action would be tantamount to committing suicide. It must be gravely doubted that such action would be taken, yet NMD proponents assert that it is likely. They need this assertion to justify NMD. It lacks rationality.

There is another puzzling aspect of the basic scenario depicted by NMD proponents. Their stance implies that the proliferation horse has bolted; indeed, it is halfway over the hill, and it is too late to take preventative action to stop it. What are the facts? Are the rogues already so advanced as to warrant a shift to a policy of cure rather than prevention? The evidence is that they are *not*.

In the light of the circumstances just discussed, NMD has all the appearances of a disproportionate response to a problem whose shape is clear and which does not warrant such a response; Pulitzer Prize–winning columnist Maureen Dowd has described it as the "Defense That Doesn't Work Against the Threat That Doesn't Exist."[16] It has the look of unilateralism gone mad. Good sense would lead to the question of what, in reality, motivates it, given that neither the claimed facts nor the rationale are credible. The likely answers to this question are disturbing.

The first is revealed in the repeated assertions by supporters of NMD that the arms control agreements cannot be relied on to prevent proliferation. As proliferation has occurred and is continuing, this would appear to be a fact-based assertion. But the situation contains more detail than this simple assertion would suggest. First, why is this the case? Second, can it be fixed? Third, what would be the consequences of giving up on this task?

Proliferation is expanding because certain states have decided to walk that path in violation of their obligations. The reasons for their decision, fully analyzed, would fill another book. In essence, however, they have been able to do so because of their certainty that the arms control regimes are not reliable. This assessment is sound from their point of view. They believe that their transgressions will go unpunished, and in reality, they do not recognize their action as a transgression because they see the present world of WMD as essentially iniquitous. As the prime case in point, they cite the continuing arrogation by the United States and other nuclear-weapon states of the right to have nuclear weapons. In the specific cases of Iran and Iraq, they are also responding to their mutual hostility, their competition in arms and influence, their deep rejection of the fact that Israel, alone in their region, should have nuclear weapons, and that this situation seems to be accepted by the United States. India and Pakistan's decisions to acquire nuclear weapons were influenced by another set of mutual concerns. These are among the many answers that can be given to the question of "why."

The question of whether these circumstances can be rectified has positive answers, although what is involved is arduous in the extreme. The decisions of rogue states to proliferate can be contained and progressively reversed first by eliminating the conviction that they will escape punishment for their actions. The preferable form of such sanctions or coercion is that it would not be exercised unilaterally by the United States. Vigorous attempts should be made to engage other nuclear-weapon states in enforcing the norms of non-proliferation, but if that failed, the United States should be prepared to make clear to rogue states that their actions are placing them in great danger and, if necessary, make good on that threat.

In parallel, the United States should act to restore credibility to the non-proliferation and nuclear disarmament processes. The International Atomic Energy Agency's safeguards system urgently needs to be strengthened, and there should be insistence that the IAEA and other relevant international inspectors be given effective access to facilities in rogue states. This could be achieved if the nuclear-weapon states and other major states resolved to make it happen. Failure to grant such access or to seek to render inspections useless should be taken as confirmation that illegal activity is taking place. The United States should work, in the first instance, with Russia to reinvigorate the nuclear disarmament process, the breakdown of which has given major support to rogue state perceptions that the non-proliferation regime is a sham.

If such actions are not taken, the consequence will be the fulfillment of that view. The international community is on the edge of that conclusion now and sees the U.S. proposal to build a NMD system as the key indicator of whether the thirty-year commitment to non-proliferation will survive. This fact needs to be understood as clearly as possible. A decision by the United States to direct its attention away from collective efforts to restrain proliferation and toward national defense is perceived as a major decision to pursue a unilateral solution to a global problem. It is seen as the arrogance and selfishness of great power without regard to its impact on others.

Such a contention will alternatively outrage or underwhelm proponents of NMD, but to exemplify it in practical terms, it could be asked, What good does it do for the other states in the Middle East if the U.S. response to Iran and Iraq's nuclear weapon acquisition plans is to build a wall around itself, having first declared that the NPT cannot be relied on and then take no action to strengthen it? This would offer no security to the Middle East, and if the NPT were to break down as a consequence, the world that would emerge would be chaotic, even for "Fortress America."

Distrust of arms control agreements is only one of the stated concerns of NMD apologists. This passivity, uncharacteristic of Americans in the face of a challenge, actually masks other possible motivations for NMD—the arrogance of great power and the possible reemergence of isolationism in America.

All that needs to be said of great power arrogance is read history. It is replete with records of great powers and empires losing influence as a consequence of the careless or arrogant use of their power. It is hard to envision this happening directly to the United States any time soon, but it would be foolish not to recognize the extent to which many countries, including those counted as friends of the United States, are anxious about the uses to which the sole superpower is putting its strength.

The United States is not invulnerable. Its extreme dependence on oil from the Middle East is a source of vulnerability and one that would be felt in U.S. domestic politics with a vengeance if the flow of oil were to be curtailed or its price sharply increased. U.S. interests are global, and it has become the single dominant economic power, but other economic groupings in Europe and Asia are growing in ways that will reduce the ability of the United States to dictate economic terms.

Introduction of the economic dimension leads again to the traditional American dalliance with isolationism, but in present circumstances, it dallies selectively. Today, the United States preaches the gospel of globalization and interdependence in the world economy, especially when others complain about the impact of the U.S. presence in their markets and economies. This is anything but isolationist. In the economic arena, the United States adopts an engaged stance because it suits its economic interests. But in its political relations, the United States is following an increasingly opposite path, with the exception of its commitment to NATO. In the political arena, it is advancing the notion of a national-interest-based foreign policy, almost implying naively that this is something new or different. All nations pursue their national interests, but the current U.S. insistence that it will start to do this *now* implies that it did not do so previously, when transparently it did.

What is being stated is that the United States proposes to heighten its recourse to narrowly defined self-interest. The stark contradiction between U.S. globalism in the world economy and what now seems likely to be its increasingly distanced relationship with the world polity is damaging. No matter how it may hanker after it, the United States cannot jump off the world. That world is a fractious, dangerous, and in-your-face place. The greatest danger it faces is nuclear weapons. Failure by the United States to engage in addressing that danger, with all of its might, would threaten itself and all others.

The specific forms of that danger inherent in a unilateral U.S. decision to build an NMD system stem from the fact that such a decision would lead other nuclear-weapons states to build more effective weapons because they could not accept the proposition that the U.S. shield would have no impact on them. This reasoning is especially true in the case of China. It does not accept the publicly stated rationale for NMD—that it is to defeat the danger posed by rogue states. Instead, it assesses that NMD is directed *at* China. Given the unconvincing nature of the administration's statements on this issue and the probable neutralizing impact of NMD on China's nuclear arsenal, this view may have some validity.

It was reported on September 2, 2001, that senior administration officials, in an attempt to neutralize China's concerns about NMD, had intimated to China that the United States would not object to China increasing the number of its nuclear missiles and that it accepted that, for this purpose, China might resume nuclear testing.[17] On the latter subject, it is also understood that the administration is considering resumption of some U.S. nuclear testing. China responded by stating that it had no intention of resuming testing, and the administration subsequently sought, unconvincingly, to clarify its position on further missile development by China, stating that it was simply accepting the reality that China planned such developments. This passage of events, together with the repeated exaggeration of the current proliferation threat to the United States, illustrates the determination of the administration to pursue NMD, irrespective of the facts.

A decision by the United States to deploy NMD would also lead to an increase in the number of states possessing nuclear weapons due to the NPT regime's breakdown.

The central reason that these unwanted events would occur is that a U.S. decision to proceed with NMD would dramatically affirm, contrary to its undertakings and against the expectation of so many states, that the United States continues to rely on its nuclear weapons as its main defense. Although this appears to have the hallmark of a status quo decision, it would, in reality, change the current world order with unpredictable consequences.

One of the first ways in which that order would change would be to provide Russia with a reason to return to what many in Russia now think were the preferable circumstances of the Cold War. Russians, far more than Americans, have felt loss and pain at the disappearance of a bipolar world. NMD could unify Russia again, and not in healthy ways.[18]

The notion of defending against deeply dangerous weapons is legitimate and appealing, perhaps especially in a popular democracy. As ever, the basic question at issue is, how can this be best achieved? It is an especially difficult question when the threat is as complex as that posed by the combustible mix of rogue states and nuclear weapons.

The claim that only NMD can provide that defense is misleading. It is not the only available means of defense, and it holds the possibility of being both intrinsically unreliable and exacerbating the very problem it sets out to resolve. With respect to the intended targets of NMD—rogue states—they are not yet at a stage of development where they could threaten the United States. More sensible action would be directed at robust measures to prevent them from reaching that stage. This is not to say that research on defense should not continue. If it resulted in the creation of technologies that would, in the words of U.S. Secretary of State Colin Powell, "devalue offensive nuclear weapons," this would be of extreme importance. The questions of how, where, and by whom it would be deployed would then take on new meaning.

Deep consideration must be given to the collateral effects of a decision to deploy unilateral NMD and to the world that would then be created. The signs are that neither would be acceptable.

The best defense against nuclear weapons, whether in the hands of established nuclear-weapon states or those that seek to acquire them, is ultimately to bring them under control and to continue to work toward their elimination. This is more than the best defense; on an enduring basis, it is the only one that will work. Although this approach may seem more difficult to achieve than a national solution, it is more certain in its outcome and less costly than the unilateral alternative.

This is the choice that must be made—between walking the hard yards of controlling the spread of nuclear weapons, and eventually eliminating them, or giving up on those goals and hunkering down to unilateral defense—the fatal choice.

6

Nuclear Security

In the nearly sixty years since the power of nuclear weapons was revealed, one central concern has motivated countries, governments, and peoples around the world—to find a way to be safe from nuclear weapons. Two routes have been followed, one by a few countries, the other by the rest.

The first, started by Stalin in response to U.S. nuclear weapons, was to obtain the same weapons. This established the nuclear arms race and the theory of deterrence through the threat of mutual assured destruction.

Russia's first nuclear detonation in 1949 was followed by the United Kingdom in 1956, France in 1960, China in 1964, and later by Israel, India, and Pakistan as the most recent nuclear-weapon states. Others, notably South Africa, and to some extent Sweden, started down the same path but later pulled back.

The second route was laid down in the Nuclear Non-Proliferation Treaty (NPT) of 1968. The safety it is intended to provide is based on preventing the spread of nuclear weapons to further countries and progressively eliminating those held by existing nuclear-weapon states.

As has already been argued, the effectiveness of the first route is dubious and unstable. It has also had the profound deficiency of causing an increase in the quantity and quality of nuclear weapons in existence. These facts justify what I believe is the axiom of proliferation: As long as any state has nuclear weapons, others will seek to acquire them.

The second route has embedded in it the worst of all nuclear nightmares—cheating from within. This is the situation where a country is a party to the NPT as a non-nuclear-weapon state but, in violation of its treaty obligations, proceeds to clandestine development of nuclear weapons.

My personal experience of the operation of the NPT and the work of the IAEA spans some thirty years. I took part repeatedly in policy-level discussions and negotiations as a representative of Australia. As Australia's special ambassador for disarmament from 1983 to 1988, I held nuclear arms control discussions in some forty countries. This experience, together with the unique one of negotiating for two years with Iraq, a country whose leader has an unparalleled record in contemporary times of acquisition and use of weapons of mass destruction, has led me to a central conclusion: The deepest anxiety held by states about the international legal regimes to prevent the proliferation of weapons of mass destruction is that the treaties may not be enforceable. The case of Iraq is seen as proof that if a state is determined enough to stick by its WMD decisions, it will prevail, because the great powers will not pay the political or material price that enforcement of treaty obligations entails.

This anxiety on the part of states that observe the non-proliferation norms is real and based on hard experience. If it is not addressed, the NPT will corrode.

Saddam Hussein's Iraq is the major case. Iraq was an original signatory to the NPT in 1968. By the mid-1970s, however, Saddam had initiated Iraq's nuclear weapons program. According to Khidhir Hamza, an Iraqi defector who worked for the clandestine program, Saddam had ordered the construction of a nuclear device as early as 1971.[1] In 1981, Israel, having become sufficiently concerned about that program and satisfied that the international community would do nothing to stop it, bombed Iraq's Osirak nuclear reactor, where nuclear weapons work was being carried out. Saddam responded by sending his program into deep cover and intensifying efforts in a "crash program" with the goal of having a nuclear weapon ready by 1991.

One outcome of the Gulf War, to expel Iraq from Kuwait, was the destruction of the crash program. Inspectors from the UN Special Commission (UNSCOM) and the International Atomic Energy Agency (IAEA) entered Iraq after the war and found that Saddam had been only six months away from completing a crude atomic weapon. One of the most dramatic confrontations, among many that occurred between Iraq and UNSCOM inspectors, was the "parking lot" standoff in September 1991. Iraqi officials held IAEA inspectors at gunpoint for four days in the parking lot of some Baghdad buildings, where they had unearthed and taken possession of extensive documentation relating to Iraq's nuclear weapons program. The inspection team was not allowed to leave the site with their records until the Security Council threatened enforcement action.

In 1998, when Iraq shut down inspections and ejected me and my team, it had still not surrendered, as it was required, key components and plans for its nuclear weapons. Since that time, it has been reliably reported that Saddam has reassembled his nuclear weapons design team. All he lacks for a nuclear weapon are the core materials. He has the know-how. There is repeated and disturbing evidence that criminal groups inside Russia have attempted to smuggle and sell those materials to him. Given his extensive black market oil operations, now yielding billions of dollars each year, he could pay an extraordinary sum for such materials. It is beyond doubt that he is willing to do so.

There are other clandestine nuclear weapon programs—in Iran and North Korea. What Iraq, Iran, and North Korea have in common is that they are members of the Nuclear Non-Proliferation Treaty. They are cheating from within; they are the embodiment of the worst nightmare.

The question of what precise purpose nuclear weapons have served is debatable. Much of what is claimed they have achieved remains speculative. If the conventional theory and structure of nuclear deterrence is accepted, then it can be argued that they prevented the Cold War from turning hot. If focus is placed more sharply on the destructive power of nuclear weapons and the necessarily theoretical foundation of deterrence, then it is more logical to conclude that through nuclear weapons we have played dice with death. What is demonstrable is that their costs have been massive, and the dangers they have held, and continue to hold, are extreme. In addition, a considerable number of those scientists who made the original nuclear weapons now believe that their creation was a mistake.

A not inconsiderable proportion of senior military commanders who during their active careers had charge of nuclear weapons now have grave reservations about their utility and primarily emphasize the dangers they pose.

Reducing reliance on nuclear weapons and working toward their elimination would change the nature of perceived threats to national and international security. That security would require protection from whatever threats are identified, including those posed by states and non-state actors seeking to rebuild or acquire nuclear weapons. The knowledge and materials required for a nuclear weapons capability would continue to exist, as is the case with other weapons that have been either abandoned through changes in technology or declared illegal.

Clearly, the elemental security problems nuclear weapons are supposed to answer still need to be addressed. They have political and other foundations that are independent from the existence of nuclear weapons, although the perception of security threat is increased in direct proportion to the quantity and quality of arms possessed by a state seen as hostile.

Alternative non-nuclear-weapon-based measures for the maintenance of security in a world of declining reliance on nuclear weapons would need to be established. Such measures could be pursued within the structure of conventional political and security relations among states. They should include new structures, both political and military, designed to respond to the unique challenge that continues to be posed by nuclear weapons, but that has never been adequately addressed.

The conduct of political relations between states is typically a long-term and sometimes tortuous business involving a complex set of competing, and sometimes hostile, interests. It is the case, however, that where such political relations are managed effectively, the need for the maintenance of a large military or defense posture between states declines.

The United States, for example, conducts its relations with a great variety of states in a detailed, highly competitive, and sometimes disputatious fashion, but at no stage feels the need to maintain a defense posture in relation to all. The number of states with which the United States maintains a relationship devoid of a military or security dimension is in the hundreds, or the substantial majority of states.

There is a small number of states, the difficult cases, against which the United States must maintain a measure of defensive capability. Although the number of such situations is relatively small, the scope of the problem is not. For decades, the maintenance of this defensive capability has required the commitment of massive resources.

An optimal design for U.S. foreign policy with respect to those few difficult states would surely begin by placing major emphasis on conducting political relations with them in a manner that would keep the need for military commitments at a lower rather than higher level. A clear analysis of the Cold War dismisses any doubt about this central proposition. The fundamental characteristic of that period in U.S.-Soviet relations was extreme hostility. The nuclear arms race resulted as a consequence.

Concerted action to greatly improve U.S. relations with other nuclear-weapon states is essential to addressing the danger posed by nuclear weapons and to a progressive reduction in the number of those weapons. The process of maintaining constructive political relations between states whose interests are considerably at variance, and who view each other with hostile opposition, is a difficult, tiresome, and long-term commitment. Moreover, it requires making clear distinctions between less than optimal situations and unacceptable positions. Living in peace with the rest of the world does not bring the obligation to like or approve of the way in which potential adversaries conduct their business or view the world. But it does mean working to establish and maintain ways of living with each other.

It is worth reflecting on the fact that relations among states in the international community are not unlike relations among individuals or groups within a democracy. In the latter case, disputes, which are inevitable, are settled by the rule of law. Although disputes are no less inevitable in international relations, recourse to law is much less reliable than in domestic society. This is because international law is much less developed than domestic law, the consent of the governed is hardly discernible, and enforcement and justice systems hardly exist. Yet, the principle of the peaceful settlement of disputes and the need to observe international law are established within the structure of contemporary international relations.

The contemporary process of negotiating arms control treaties has three main elements.

First, *agreement is reached among states on a norm of behavior,* such as that no state should possess or use a specified type of weapon. This is the case today with respect to nuclear, chemical, and biological weapons.

The force or specificity with which such norms of behavior are expressed varies. In the case of nuclear weapons, some contend that the NPT does not specifically provide that no state should possess nuclear weapons. Such persons illustrate their case by pointing out that, by contrast, the same is not true with respect to the treaties on chemical and biological weapons.

As I have already argued, however, the NPT can be taken as stating, as a norm, that no state should have nuclear weapons because of the obligations it places on those who do not have them to never acquire them and on those who have such arsenals to eliminate them.

What can be concluded from this is that the norms stated in the major weapons of mass destruction treaties are expressed in varying ways and may lend themselves to varying interpretations. But the establishment of a norm is the first, indeed necessary, condition of a viable arms control treaty. The norm is arrived at through political negotiation, but once agreed upon, it then assumes the character of a high, if not moral, principle.

Second, principles are all very fine as affirmed by philosophers or extolled from the pulpit, but in a world of sovereign states, they are given life in the text of a treaty that states choose to join or not. *The negotiation of a treaty—a contract among states—sets out how the principle will work in practice.* Because the treaty is seen as establishing the rights and duties of states, the negotiation of its text becomes a trenchant political struggle in which every word and comma is beaten into shape.

When a text is agreed upon, the major exercise of sovereignty awaits. Each state is free to decide to sign or not to sign. In the cases of the Nuclear Non-Proliferation Treaty, the Biological Weapons Convention, and the Chemical Weapons Convention, the overwhelming majority of states have signed.

Third, *a means of verification of state compliance with treaty obligations is established* and written into the treaty to make it work and, above all, to provide assurance to treaty partners. Typically provided are scientific examination and inspections so that verification can be made that any given state is adhering to its treaty obligations.

Although verification is technical and apparently objective in nature, the negotiation of verification regimes, and their subsequent practical application, is very much overshadowed by political considerations. It must be noted, in this context, that the Biological Weapons Convention does not yet have a verification protocol—for political reasons. The United States has rejected the current draft verification protocol, claiming that it would not be effective and would result in the loss of U.S. scientific intellectual property. It is not clear how, if it is the former, it could result in the latter.

Two things can be said of this three-part process: It is more developed today than at any previous time; and it is inherently political even though much of what is dealt with is material, technical, and able to be largely objectified through accurate measurement of numbers and types of weapons.

The disarmament treaty foundation has three legs. Like any tripod, it can be stable but never as stable as a four-legged stand. The fourth leg, required for the platform of WMD arms control to be secure, is a reliable means of enforcement of obligations, of remedying infractions, of demonstrating to the whole community, as is regularly done in domestic law, that a criminal will be stopped and punished.

Each of the WMD non-proliferation treaties contains references to the right of treaty partners to withdraw from the treaty and to action that might be contemplated against a state that remains in the treaty but clandestinely commences cheating on it. The former case serves to signal to the community that a state intends to break the treaty norm. Undesirable though any such decision may be, notice of it enables others to consider what this action means and what might be done about it. As pointed out earlier, the nightmarish latter scenario has occurred in the case of Iraq. Such situations are, under present political arrangements, extremely difficult to remedy. A proposal to change this, to construct the fourth leg, is addressed below.

What is important now is to underline that the WMD arms control treaties are constituent parts of international law, and all state members of the United Nations are obliged to conduct themselves in accordance with international law. Important elements of the modern body of international law relevant to nuclear weapons are the obligation to avoid the use of excessive force, the necessity of avoiding harm to non-combatants in armed conflict, and the commitment to the elimination of nuclear weapons.

When political discussions on establishing a world free of nuclear weapons are held, they are very often met with objections asserting that disarmed nuclear-weapon states could be held hostage by rogue states clandestinely possessing other weapons of mass destruction. It is beyond doubt that this anxiety gives expression to a set of real and, in some instances, growing problems. These concerns require a solution if advanced nuclear arms control and the eventual elimination of nuclear weapons are to be achieved.

Action designed to reduce and then eliminate the nuclear danger must therefore be accompanied by the maintenance of collective security structures that can provide peace, security, and stability in a world of diminished reliance on nuclear weapons. Much of that framework already exists in the WMD arms control treaties. What has been lacking up until the present, indeed has been glaringly absent, is the determination to ensure that those treaties do their job.

A new security structure would need to ensure that WMD arms control treaties were strengthened and universally applied. For this to be achieved, the major powers would need to take specific steps, including political action to secure universal participation in the NPT and to strengthen the IAEA safeguards system, the establishment of a verification mechanism for the Biological Weapons Convention, and further development of controls over trade in the materials and technologies of weapons of mass destruction. The major powers would also need to conduct themselves in ways consistent with these requirements. For example, they could not expect others to refrain from exporting WMD-related materials and technology if they did not do the same.

The new instrument that would be required would be a mechanism for the enforcement of the relevant WMD treaties and arrangements. This would require political agreement among the major states to establish, empower, and support such a mechanism, including the maintenance of the required conventional military forces and readiness for enforcement tasks.

Given the nature, power, and sophistication of modern conventional weapons technology, the threat of collective military action with such weapons would be sufficient to ensure that an enforcement mechanism would be effective. It would not be necessary for any nuclear weapons to be maintained as a part of that enforcement capability. This would avoid the inherent and destructive contradiction that would flow from any proposal that had as its ultimate goal the elimination of nuclear weapons, but that included the retention of a quantity of nuclear weapons in order to ensure enforcement of global nuclear arms control arrangements. It must also be remembered in this context that the idea of asymmetrical deterrence—the notion that a WMD attack by a state or non-state actor could be deterred by the threat of nuclear weapons—is specious.

The maintenance of national and, by extension, international security is avowedly complex and costly under any circumstance. The problems involved are inherently dynamic. They include deep and shifting anxieties about national security and, very often, the even more incalculable concepts of prestige, nation, and mission.

There is also the fundamental problem of equity among states, which reaches its height in the assertion by nuclear-weapon states that national security requires the maintenance of such weapons, but that this does not apply to the vast majority of states.

What follows from this is that efforts to maintain security in a world freed from nuclear weapons would be equally large and complex. Action would need to be taken on a sustained basis on all fronts—political, military, and legal. It would entail the development of a new concept of collective action in international relations and a new legal basis for it. The financial costs would be high, but significantly lower than the present outlays for the maintenance of nuclear weapons systems.

Meeting this challenge requires states to organize politically and militarily in new ways. Established habits in the conduct of international relations need to be adapted to this special case. Established habits alone lead, as they appear to be doing now, to heightened reliance on unilateral defense, which asserts that states must defend themselves because there is no way of preventing criminal activity.

The NPT provides for a system under which infractions or matters of concern under the treaty are reported to the United Nations Security Council, but this body has repeatedly shown itself unwilling or unable to take the kind of action that is so deeply required and on which most states rely. The system of referring infractions to the Security Council is deeply flawed. The main source of that flaw does not lie within the provisions of the NPT, the effectiveness of verification, or the controls over transfers of relevant materials and technology. Rather, it lies within the nature and methodology of the Security Council itself. Specifically, when one of the five permanent members of the Council—China, France, Russia, the United Kingdom, or the United States—declines to agree to a proposal of substance, as in a proposal to take enforcement action against a state in breach of its NPT obligations, the proposal is not adopted. This is known as the veto, a power held by each of these five permanent members. This is not a technical or scientific matter; it is politics in its purest form. The possibility that any one of the five permanent members of the Security Council could veto such action is precisely what renders enforcement of NPT obligations unreliable.

The remedy to this situation lies in a political agreement among the five permanent members, which are, of course, also the acknowledged nuclear-weapon states under the terms of the NPT. They must agree that the veto will not be deployed whenever a reliably reported infraction of obligations under the NPT comes before them and that they will collectively take action to remedy the reported situation.

Such an agreement would constitute a major political decision to make enforcement of the NPT an exception from the normal veto procedures of the Security Council. If those holding that veto considered this to be an unacceptable intrusion into their powers within the Security Council, or its working methods, it could be dealt with through the establishment of a separate body with a similar constituency, but with a specific mandate to protect non-proliferation norms.

For this purpose, a Council on Weapons of Mass Destruction, on which a representative group of relevant states would sit, should be established. It would have the role of monitoring progress in the implementation and enforcement of the WMD arms control mechanisms. With respect to nuclear weapons, the council would consider reports under the NPT and make decisions on enforcement of treaty obligations, as necessary. It would have assigned to it powers of enforcement similar to those set forth in Article 42 of the Charter of the United Nations, which provides the powers of enforcement to the Security Council with respect to its own decisions. Article 42 states that the Security Council "may take such action by air, sea, or land forces as may be necessary to maintain or restore international peace and security. Such action may include demonstrations, blockade, and other operations by air, sea, or land forces of Members of the United Nations."

The Council would need expert advice. A secretariat would need to be established composed substantially of persons with relevant technical expertise. It would furnish the council with the facts of any given case of possible non-compliance by a state with its non-proliferation obligations.

The sources of information available to the secretariat would include materials provided by treaty bodies and organizations such as the International Atomic Energy Agency and national intelligence organizations. It may need, itself, to have powers of inspection of and discussion with states.

The establishment of such a body would clearly involve contentious negotiations among states, but their interest in making such arrangements may be identified in the degree of objectivity that would be introduced into the assembly of data, which, if left entirely to political negotiation, would almost never emerge without damaging distortion.

Critics of this proposal could be expected to argue that it would lead to repeated large and costly military interventions in defense of the NPT. This underassesses the impact of a decision by the great powers to make an exception from politics as usual for nuclear arms control. Where under the usual politics they would be almost inevitably divided, under this proposal, with their mandate specifically made to support compliance with the NPT, their only division would be over the meaning of factual reports of state compliance with the NPT and proposed remedial action. Such divisions would not be supported by veto power. This would limit the scope for division leading to inaction. And the scope for division on factual matters would be small, assuming the data put to them was accurate.

If such stark political resistance from the five nuclear-weapon states to breaches of the NPT were reliable, the occasions on which a state would be willing to cheat would decline steadily. It is unlikely that military intervention would be required frequently, if at all, and such intervention would not need to involve a large-scale war with the country concerned. The threat of military action targeted at the offending scientific and technical facilities would be sufficient in almost all instances.

With respect to other WMD treaties, the existing treaty mechanisms could continue to operate. For example, the International Atomic Energy Agency could continue its work under the Nuclear Non-Proliferation Treaty and the Organization for the Prevention of Chemical Weapons could continue to develop its work. But the existing ambiguity about what action would be taken in the event of breakout or breakdown would be removed by a Council on WMD. As long as any state intent upon criminal activity has reason to believe that nothing adverse will result from proceeding with that activity, it will have no incentive to desist. Any such state would need to think again if the possibility of action to enforce WMD norms was seen to be strong and reliable.

The existence of a Council on Weapons of Mass Destruction would provide an important forum for consideration, discussion, and debate on the reasons a given state had embarked upon the acquisition of nuclear weapons. Were such a state to be called to the bar of the council and confronted with information that could possibly lead to the threat of enforcement action, it would be given the opportunity to both deal with the factual materials at issue and explain what was motivating its decision to acquire nuclear weapons. This would provide the international community with the opportunity to address the political and security concerns that allegedly motivated the acquisition decision. It would also provide the opportunity for such motivation to be exposed, especially when it was essentially aggressive or imperialist rather than rooted in what might be considered to be legitimate national security concerns. Thus, action to expose clandestine nuclear weapons development could itself retard such development.

At this point, it must be recognized that no collective action by the nuclear-weapon states would be credible or perhaps possible if they were themselves in breach of their own NPT obligations. The irreducible argument of equity remains at issue. For such a council to succeed and for the threat of enforcement to be credible, the nuclear-weapon states would need to demonstrate that they were themselves working, in the words of the treaty, "in good faith" toward the elimination of their own nuclear weapons, a promise they reiterated in their common statement of May 2000.

It has already been argued that the NPT should be seen as supplementing the UN Charter, forming an integral part of the structure of contemporary international relations. A Council on Weapons of Mass Destruction capable of enforcing the NPT obligations, in a way analogous to the role of the Security Council under the UN Charter, would strengthen that structure.

Given the special nature of the problems posed by WMD, it is appropriate for a Council on Weapons of Mass Destruction to have assigned to it the authority to enforce agreed upon norms and standards under WMD treaties. It could be argued that such authority already exists in the Security Council, but the existence and habit of the veto power within that body makes it unreliable for this crucial WMD task. The charter for a new Council on Weapons of Mass Destruction could remove that deficiency while preserving the established functions and decisionmaking methodologies of the Security Council. What is at root in this proposal is recognition of the tested fact that if a job is to be done on a subject of special character, then it is done best by establishing specific arrangements and resources for that purpose.

To proceed in this way would represent and require something of a shift in the mentality that was established at the end of World War II and throughout the Cold War, a mentality that included the view that the possession of weapons of mass destruction was essential to the national security interests of specific states. This thinking is proving to be a dangerous failure.

Our choice is either to await a catastrophe that would demonstrate the truth of that failure in wholly undesirable ways or to head it off now by making the arrangements that were not made originally when the United Nations was formed in 1945. Such arrangements could not be made then, since there was little understanding of what the world of weapons of mass destruction would become. There is no such lack of understanding today. It needs to be translated into action.

The post–World War II security architecture established the Security Council as its keystone. The post–Cold War architecture needs another such rock—the Council on Weapons of Mass Destruction.

Plan of Action

I have often found that thoughts darken around midnight. At that hour, one cold evening in Geneva in 1985, following a tortuous day at the Nuclear Non-Proliferation Treaty Review Conference, I sat in my living room with David Fischer. For more than twenty years, he had done more than any other person to make the treaty effective. David was a refugee from apartheid South Africa. He had left his country's diplomatic service thirty years earlier in protest against the racist policies of his beloved country. He then became an official of the newly established International Atomic Energy Agency (IAEA), where he rose to become its deputy director general. Ironically, he could never attain the top job *because* he was a South African, notwithstanding the actions he had taken to condemn apartheid.

My living room, with only one sidelight burning, was as dark as my mood, and a squall outside on the surface of Lake Leman completed the atmospherics. I complained to David about the subterfuge, the games, and the antics that were being played out at the conference. Everything was being tried by the main protagonists to avoid the central issue—reductions in nuclear weapons.

David agreed, and then he told me a story, perhaps all the more fitting as he came from a land rich in wild animals.

It was of a meeting of the Royal Zoological Society in London that had taken place a couple of hundred years earlier. An expedition had brought back from some distant corner of the globe an animal never seen before, something like a Komodo dragon. Its main characteristic, apart from being utterly unknown, was its fearsome and ugly appearance. It was gnarled, slimy, and had a hideous color and texture. It seemed to stink; it was possibly poisonous. It was placed on a table in the very center of the meeting room, so that it could be examined.

The Royal Society's meetings always followed a careful protocol. There was much courtesy and decorum. This was especially so when its leading personalities were assembled, as was the case, David assured me, on this occasion. As David made this point, I thought—just like diplomacy.

The meeting lasted a couple of hours, and remarkably, no one present referred to the beast in the room, no one touched or examined it. Eyes were rigidly averted. Every other conceivable subject of zoology was discussed, but not the beast. The meeting ended, and everyone went off into the night.

David's story, true or not, has remained with me. It was so appropriate to our circumstances that night and at that time in Geneva. It has numerous interpretations. Were the distinguished participants at the Royal Zoological Society silently united in their individual wish to conceal their ignorance of the beast?

Or, was it that the beast was too horrible to examine? Were they simply afraid?

What I have thought subsequently, as I have taken part in countless arms control meetings, is that nuclear weapons are the beast in the center of the room. If we are going to succeed in controlling them, we will need to grasp them, directly.

UN Undersecretary General for Disarmament Affairs Jayantha Dhanapala, a member of the Canberra Commission on the Elimination of Nuclear Weapons, recently reflected on this central requirement: "The ultimate challenge to the global nuclear non-proliferation regime . . . is to sustain and expand the foundation of political support for the goals for which it stands—namely, the elimination of nuclear weapons in the interest of international peace and security, and non-proliferation as a stepping-stone to that goal."[1]

Dhanapala, like Fischer, has worked in the nuclear arms control field at senior levels for more than twenty-five years. As a young diplomat from Sri Lanka, he trained in my training year, 1966, in the Australian Foreign Service. Perhaps in spite of that, he is a very wise man. He presided over the 1995 NPT Review and Extension Conference and was one of the sixteen people at my dinner table, where agreement on the treaty's indefinite extension was reached.

The arrangements made among nations for the control of nuclear weapons have been progressively and carefully built over a period of some forty years. The resultant structure is uneven, anything but neat, yet it has proven effective in most respects. This fact makes it all the more wanton and damaging for those who now want to bypass the structure, to exaggerate its weaknesses, indeed to condemn it as if it were a building unable to be repaired, in order to justify building a U.S. national missile defense shield.

Integral to such criticism have been a misrepresentation of facts, such as the extraordinary degree of compliance the NPT has attracted, and a conscious choice to interpret instances of cheating as proof that the NPT is a failure. The exceptions are being interpreted as the rule.

It is important to recognize that extant arrangements to prevent the proliferation of nuclear weapons are not faultless, but the question this should raise, in all logic, is whether the faults at issue are indeed fundamental and thus irreparable.

The stated policy position of the United States is that it views the NPT as "the cornerstone of the international nuclear non-proliferation regime and the essential foundation for nuclear disarmament"[2] and that it remains "unequivocally committed to fulfilling all of [its] obligations under the Treaty."[3] Given these commitments, and the dictates of sound logic, the answer the United States should give to the question of whether the regime should be fixed or scrapped is clearly the former.

Road maps for that work were agreed to by the United States and the other nuclear-weapon states at both the 1995 NPT Review and Extension Conference and again at the 2000 NPT Review Conference.[4] There is no lack of awareness of what needs to be done to strengthen the NPT regime. What has been absent is adequate work to implement the steps so defined and agreed upon.

A careful scrutiny of the agreed-upon statement by the nuclear-weapon states of May 1, 2000, reveals that on the key issues of their own obligations under the NPT and their new promise to eliminate nuclear weapons, the best they have been able to commit to in practice is "to take a forward-looking approach to nuclear non-proliferation and nuclear disarmament."[5]

The agreed-upon statement contains other curiosities such as a declaration "that none of our nuclear weapons are targeted at any state"[6] and a commitment to "preserving and strengthening the ABM Treaty as a cornerstone of strategic stability and a basis for further reductions of strategic offensive weapons, in accordance with its provisions."[7] If the administration in Washington were to fulfill its reported intention to withdraw from the ABM Treaty, that action would, among other effects, abrogate this latter aspect of the joint declaration. This would be a breach of faith with all members of the Nuclear Non-Proliferation Treaty.

The current and possibly prevailing outlook in Washington toward the NPT regime can be compressed into two essential elements. First, there is a manifest gap between U.S. diplomatic rhetoric and its behavior. The fact of such a gap could be seen to be unremarkable, for a variety of reasons, and to be fair, the United States is not alone in this. All of the nuclear weapon states are in roughly similar positions. France, for example, is currently developing a new generation of nuclear-weapon capable missiles and has apparently felt no sense of restraint flowing from its participation in the May 2000 declaration. Russia has increased its reliance on nuclear weapons since May 2000. What is crucial about this gap, however, is the damage it continues to cause to the NPT regime. This introduces the second issue.

Every such step, every instance of clear abuse of NPT obligations, both in practice and rhetoric, retards the process of work on strengthening the regime. This sets up a circle of defeat: The regime is unreliable; we must therefore take our own actions to defend against the outcomes of that unreliability; but those unilateral actions further increase the alleged unreliability of the regime, and so on. This circle must be broken. If it is not, the whole enterprise of nuclear arms control will degrade and ultimately perish.

It is evident that the current U.S. administration is imbued with an extreme, negative attitude toward international law and treaties. The Bush administration's resolution of the key conflict that exists between the notion of national sovereignty, which is fundamental in international law, and the duty of states to fulfill the terms of the international agreements and treaties into which it has entered is always to find in favor of the former. This view is extended to the point where some members of the Bush administration assert that there is, in fact, no such thing as international law; there is only national sovereignty.

Ideologically satisfying though that stance may be, it is plainly dishonest. The United States participates in a whole panoply of international laws daily—laws regulating trade, communications, aviation, passage on the high seas, diplomatic relations, to name only a minor portion of relevant agreements and conventions. The United States is unhesitating in taking recourse to law when its interests have been jeopardized, for example, to protect its nationals and its commerce.

What the extreme view held in the Bush administration expresses is nothing more than a pathetic selfishness—the wish to arbitrarily pick and choose between portions of international law, which at any given time it sees as favoring its interests or impeding them. One member of the administration, U.S. State Department Director for Policy Planning Richard Haas, has described this stance as "à la carte multilateralism." Others in the Bush administration have justified the approach because the United States is the sole superpower and is therefore exceptional.

Contrast this stance with U.S. domestic law, where a vast industry exists within the United States directed at seeking to bend, find loopholes in, and seek advantageous applications of the law for individuals. This often leads to changes in the law, but it rarely challenges the notion of the very existence of law as a mainstay of civilized society, other than by persons of an anarchist cast of mind, such as the Oklahoma City bomber, Timothy McVeigh.

A current key example of the United States placing itself outside the ambit of international law, as distinct from disagreeing with its specific formulation as it has a sovereign right to do, is its refusal to sign the Statute for the International Criminal Court on the ground that it would not be prepared to allow any American to be brought before the International Court. Its objections to the statute could be remedied under the provisions of the statute. It could also seek to gain acceptance of amendments to the statute. Both of these actions would constitute an exercise of U.S. sovereignty. Instead, its current attitude implies that American norms and values are distinct from or possibly superior to norms and values widely agreed to by the community of nation-states. It surely cannot imply that no American could ever commit the crimes over which the International Criminal Court would have jurisdiction. That would be truly preposterous. It is also a deeply disturbing stance given the role the United States played in the establishment and conduct of the trials of Nazi war criminals at Nuremberg and in the pending trial of Slobodan Milosevic at the International Criminal Tribunal for the former Yugoslavia.

In the case of nuclear weapons, the United States has exercised its sovereignty in becoming a party to the NPT. It has benefited from that decision and the operation of the treaty. Its membership has also brought it obligations. It has failed to fulfill them, as indeed have the other nuclear-weapon states. This selective attitude toward the balance of rights and duties established in the NPT jeopardizes its existence. U.S. interests are deeply involved, and they are not adequately addressed by an extremist view of the nature of international law or mere rhetoric about its intentions under the NPT.

One extreme answer to the problem of the gap between rhetoric and action would be to abandon the rhetoric. That could have the virtue of honesty, but it would have nothing else to recommend it.

Imagine the circumstances if the United States or other nuclear-weapon states were to say: "We've been lying. We have no intention of ending our reliance on nuclear weapons. We will not fulfill our commitment under Article VI of the NPT, but we will continue to expect non-nuclear-weapon states to fulfill theirs of never acquiring nuclear weapons." It would be a toss-up between which reaction would come faster or in larger measure—the beginnings of nuclear weapons programs in a number of countries or a major breakdown in global political relations. What *is* certain is that both would occur.

Hyperbolic though this conjecture might seem, in fact, it is not. There are individuals in nuclear-weapon state capitals who resent the restraints of the NPT. During the 1995 and 2000 NPT review conferences, there were corridor mutterings among non-nuclear-weapon states about resigning from or suspending their membership in the treaty in protest against nuclear-weapon state conduct. The main reason they did not take such action was because they became aware that there were groups in nuclear-weapon state capitals who would welcome the suspension of the NPT.

A hard-nosed assessment of a full-fledged breakdown in the NPT would surely lead, even if reluctantly, to the conclusion that such a development would not be in the national interests of the United States. The NPT may be something of a hair shirt to the nuclear-weapon states, but the sensible conclusion is that, itchy though it is, it protects against some very ill and chilly winds.

These circumstances call for a new policy in support of nuclear arms control. The existing arrangements for that control have faced a growing crisis for at least a decade. The matters at issue are more important to all humanity than virtually any other of the many problems nations and peoples face today.

One of the gravest of those problems, nationally and internationally, is the traffic in, and use of, narcotic drugs. It is a phenomenon, in a number of respects, not unlike the international arms trade. Arms, especially weapons of mass destruction, certainly have their addicts, of which Saddam Hussein is an example.

If the current U.S. administration were to apply to nuclear weapons the same approach it applies to narcotics—that of zero tolerance and "war on drugs"—because of their extreme danger to civilized society, the United States would surely join the ranks of the most determined nuclear weapon abolitionists.

What differentiates the two approaches? Is it held that narcotics are more threatening to life and social order than nuclear weapons, their proliferation, the doctrine of mutual assured destruction? Or is it that one goal—the abolition of narcotics—is seen as more within reach than the elimination of nuclear weapons or simply closer to homes and electorates?

Both areas are difficult, no doubt, but the idea that the problems of nuclear weapons, and the dangers they pose, are more distant and overall under better control than those of the now ubiquitous and growing use of narcotics is not supported by the facts. Nuclear weapons simply *appear* less immediately threatening in the daily lives of families than do narcotics, but clearly they *are* present, around the clock, many on hair-trigger alert.

The new strategies and resources required to prevent the spread of nuclear weapons, and to move safely toward their elimination, would be less costly than those required for narcotics and would have more certain results. What has been absent is the will to make that commitment. This is all the more tragic because nuclear arms control is an area redolent with proof of the principle that when a solution to a serious problem is postponed, its ultimate solution becomes more costly. The cost of the proposed national missile defense demonstrates this.

What is required is a comprehensive U.S. policy. The present situation of nuclear arms control cannot be remedied by tinkering, by incremental steps addressed to pieces of the problem. Those pieces, each intrinsically important, interact and necessarily so because the thread that binds them is the existence of nuclear weapons anywhere. Nothing would contribute more to further breakdown in nuclear arms control than a continuation of the attempt to deny this linkage, to assert, no matter how implicitly, that U.S. nuclear weapons are somehow different from, or more justifiable than, those of any other state, now or in the future.

The United States does not have a whole, unitary nuclear arms control policy. Adding up the sum of its parts—the U.S.-Russian piece, the deterrence-defense doctrines, the non-proliferation policy—would not constitute a coherent whole, no matter how vigorously it was declared to be the case. Any person who has dealt with successive U.S. administrations on these issues, as I have at a senior level for more than twenty years, is aware of the absence of seamlessness and the presence of major contradictions among the elements of U.S. policy. I have seen this take the almost laughable form of U.S. representatives advancing very different positions within the same hour within the same international negotiation. I repeatedly experienced U.S. officials telling me privately, "Don't take seriously what our representative is now saying publicly. Believe me; what I'm telling you is our real position."

Such minor but telling detail aside, the time is now, ripened perhaps especially by the administration's commitment to national missile defense, for the United States to announce with crystal clarity where it stands on nuclear weapons and where it proposes it and other states should travel.

A whole policy would address the full range of central issues in nuclear arms control: reinvigoration of nuclear disarmament; prevention of the emergence of new nuclear-weapon states and the acquisition of nuclear weapons by non-state or terrorist groups; and the development of an enforcement mechanism to ensure that safety and security are preserved in a world of ever diminishing reliance on nuclear weapons. The only way in which this could be achieved is for the United States to initiate and lead the articulation and implementation of a plan of action for future nuclear arms control.

If the United States proposed such a plan, it could accommodate its continuing work on measures to defend itself against ballistic missiles and possibly relieve it from the not incredible charge that its nuclear defense proposals signaled its unilateral abandonment of its commitment to global nuclear arms control. It needs to be noted that theater missile defense, as distinct from an overarching strategic system, does not and should not raise any of these problems. Its development should be seen within the construct of the basic right to defense, particularly of armed forces in the field.

Plan of Action

The plan of action outlined stated below is divided into five main parts. The first of these, a comprehensive policy declaration and associated actions by the United States, is crucial. Every other step relies on this first step.

1. Policy Declaration

The president of the United States should make a major policy statement on nuclear weapons and the actions the United

States itself proposes to take and those it proposes to take in conjunction with others.

It should call upon all states to join the United States in a major effort to solve the problem of nuclear weapons, finally. That statement should begin by recognizing the dangers posed to all by nuclear weapons and then establish the case for new action on those dangers. It should then proceed to identify the steps the United States will take. Those steps would fall under four headings: unilateral actions, bilateral actions, multilateral actions, and the establishment of a new mechanism for the maintenance of global security in circumstances of diminishing reliance upon nuclear weapons.

The president should also directly appeal to the people of the United States to support his initiative. This initiative together with the actions to be taken to rid the world of terrorism following the attack on the United States on September 11, 2001, should become defining actions to secure their future and shape the twenty-first century.

2. Unilateral Actions

On the political level, the United States should make clear that it will elevate the issue of compliance with the established norms on nuclear weapons, and the cooperation by states with future nuclear arms control objectives, to the level of first-rank importance in bilateral political and security relations between the United States and all other states. Those relations would be affected centrally by state performance on nuclear arms control.

The United States should ratify immediately its accession to the Comprehensive Nuclear Test Ban Treaty (CTBT) and take vigorous action to achieve the ratification of that treaty by all of those states required for its entry into force.

With respect to the planned development of measures for national missile defense, the United States should make clear that it proposes to continue research on the development of such defensive measures. It should state that it will discuss with all relevant states any decision by it to implement such measures and that it will consider the possibility of sharing defensive measures with relevant states.

It should make clear that in instances where states prove unprepared to participate actively in the measures of enhanced nuclear arms control outlined in U.S. policy, any role they might be permitted to play in discussion of national missile defense issues would be reduced, if not eliminated.

The United States should make clear that it will pursue, as a matter of the right to self-defense, the development of theater missile defense technologies.

3. Bilateral Actions

The United States should enter immediately into negotiations with Russia on a new strategic arms reduction treaty aiming for a reduction in the strategic nuclear weapons held by each side to a figure around or below 1,000 such weapons.

At the onset of these negotiations, the United States and Russia should reach agreement on ending the hair-trigger alert status on which their strategic nuclear weapons are currently maintained.

The United States and Russia should move immediately to eliminate all other nuclear weapons, the superfluous non-strategic stocks held by each.

The United States and Russia should reach agreement on the conditions for and time at which they would invite all other nuclear-weapon states to enter into negotiations with them on the progressive reduction of all nuclear weapons.

4. Multilateral Actions

The United States should set into effect, with other nuclear-weapons states and other relevant states, action on the thirteen steps agreed to at the 2000 Review Conference on the NPT.[8] Key actions would include the following:

- the early conclusion of a treaty ending any further production of weapons-grade fissile material,
- the development of new mechanisms for the control over trade in materials, technology, and information relevant to the development of nuclear weapons,
- the strengthening of the safeguards system of the International Atomic Energy Agency, and
- action to bring about universal membership of the NPT.

Outside the area of nuclear weapons, the United States would assign priority to actions to accomplish the following:

- bringing to an early conclusion the negotiation of verification arrangements under the Biological Weapons Convention,
- strengthening the missile technology control regime, and
- increasing support for the implementation of the chemical weapons convention.

5. New Mechanisms

The United States should propose the establishment of a Council on Weapons of Mass Destruction. For this purpose it should draw up an outline of the responsibilities and powers of such a council. It should provide that outline to all states and then convene a diplomatic conference on the establishment of that council and the creation of a charter for it, including its secretariat.

As a part of that consultation, the United States should call for the establishment of a multilateral enforcement mechanism designed to provide reliable enforcement action against states that are determined to violate the norms with respect to nuclear weapons and, as appropriate, other weapons of mass destruction.

In these two contexts, consideration would also be given to the specific challenges posed by possible action by non-state or terrorist groups possessing or seeking to acquire nuclear explosive capability. This could take into account existing law and agreements with respect to terrorism but should also aim to develop specific measures of cooperation to identify such

terrorist activity and to take multilateral enforcement action
against it.

*   *   *

Is such a plan of action too great a leap, too much, too radical a
step to ask of a new president whose senior advisors were
shaped by the Cold War period and who has emphasized repeatedly that his constant criterion for judging any matter of
foreign or security policy is the national interest of the United
States, not obeisance to externally derived principles?

No, it is not, precisely because what is proposed would give
effect to a central U.S. interest in the area of national security—the prevention of the proliferation of nuclear weapons
and, as Secretary of State Colin Powell has put it, the reduction
in the value of offensive nuclear weapons. There would be
other very considerable benefits to President George W. Bush:
the act and fact of leadership, the reshaping of history, the creation of a safer world.

The president would be counseled against this action,
warned of extreme dangers, urged to hasten slowly. The most
seductive argument would, in fact, be the worst one—that the
United States is the most powerful country in the world, so why
should it be concerned about the nuclear weapons aspirations
of others that are distant, and a light-year behind the United
States technologically? Surely, it would be more effective to
simply build U.S. defenses.

Care would have to be exercised with that argument since,
after all, it is precisely to those distant, backward countries that

NMD is allegedly addressed. At the every least, its proponents would have a problem with consistency of argument. Far worse, U.S. credibility would be low and its selfishness condemned, precisely because of its great power.

If such reasoning were to succeed, it would first have to misrepresent the facts of the relationship between U.S. conduct as a nuclear-weapon state party to the NPT and the prospect of continued adherence of non-nuclear-weapon states to their NPT undertakings. It would need to assert that there is no such relationship when clearly there is one.

Vastly more important, such reasoning would seek to deny to the president the potential power he holds, uniquely, to lead and shape the twenty-first century. This would do him and all of us a great disservice. It would make him appear to be among the smallest of men.

President Eisenhower's farewell address, forty years ago, bears recollection again: "America's leadership and prestige depend, not merely upon our unmatched material progress, riches and military strength, but on how we use our power in the interests of world peace and human betterment."[9]

A decision by President George W. Bush to make the choice for nuclear survival, and not the fatal choice, would be supported and trusted by the great majority of the American people because it would be the right choice and would be made by the president, reflecting clear "understanding lodged inside the human head."[10]

It would ensure the future of the United States and the world.

NOTES

Preface

1. Richard Butler, *The Greatest Threat: Iraq, Weapons of Mass Destruction, and the Crisis of Global Security*, (New York: Public Affairs, 2000), xix–xxi.

Chapter 1

1. "Farewell Radio and Television Address to the American People, January 17, 1961," in *Public Papers of the Presidents of the United States: Dwight D. Eisenhower, 1960–1961* (Washington, D.C.: Office of the Federal Register, 1961), 1039.

Chapter 2

1. See the detailed analysis in Stephen I. Schwartz, *Atomic Audit: The Costs and Consequences of U.S. Nuclear Weapons Since 1940* (Washington, D.C.: Brookings Institution Press, 1998).

2. Ibid., 5.

3. Valentin Tikhonov, *Russia's Nuclear and Missile Complex: The Human Factor in Proliferation* (Washington, D.C.: Carnegie Endowment for International Peace, 2001).

4. Atomic Energy Commission, Department of Defense, "The Effects of Nuclear Weapons," 1962. Available at: http://www.cdi.org/Issues/NukeAccidents/accidents.html.

5. U.S. Department of Defense, "Narrative Summaries of Accidents Involving U.S. Nuclear Weapons, 1950–1980," April 1981. Text available at: http://www.fas.org/irp/congress/1992 cr/s920803-ctbt.htm.

6. Center for Defense Information. Available at: http://www.cdi.org/Issues/NukeAccidents/accidents.html.

7. R. Bynum, "Somewhere off the Georgia Coast, a Cold War Relic Rests," *Associated Press*, 21 January 2001.

8. William M. Arkin and Hans Kristensen, "Dangerous Directions," *Bulletin of the Atomic Scientists*, March/April 1998; R. Jeffrey Smith, "Clinton Directive Changes Strategy on Nuclear Arms," *Washington Post*, 7 December 1997, A1.

9. Bruce Blair, "START III, Nuclear War Plans and the Cold War Mindset," *Defense Monitor*, Vol. 29, No. 5, 2000. Available at: www.cdi.org/dm/2000/issue5/start.html.

Chapter 3

1. UN General Assembly Resolution 1 (I), "The Establishment of a Commission to Deal with the Problems Raised by the Discovery of Atomic Energy," adopted on 24 January 1946, called for "the elimination from national armaments of atomic weapons and of all other major weapons adaptable to mass destruction."

2. Article I of the Charter of the United Nations.

3. The Universal Declaration on Human Rights was adopted by the General Assembly of the United Nations (without dissent) on 10 December 1948.

4. UN document A/51/218, para. 105, 15 October 1996.

5. UN General Assembly Resolution 49/75 K, "Request for an Advisory Opinion from the International Court of Justice on the Legality of the Threat or Use of Nuclear Weapons," 15 December 1994.

6. UN General Assembly Resolution 1380 (XIV).

7. UN General Assembly Resolution 1665 (XVI).

8. John F. Kennedy, "The President's News Conference of March 21, 1963," in *Public Papers of the Presidents of the United States: John F. Kennedy, 1963* (Washington, D.C.: Office of the Federal Register, 1964), 280.

9. UN General Assembly Resolution 2028 (XX).

10. Article I of the Treaty on the Non-Proliferation of Nuclear Weapons (1968).

11. Article II of the Treaty on the Non-Proliferation of Nuclear Weapons (1968).

12. Article VI of the Treaty on the Non-Proliferation of Nuclear Weapons (1968).

13. Article II of the Statute of the IAEA.

14. Article VI of the Treaty on the Non-Proliferation of Nuclear Weapons (1968).

15. Preamble of the Treaty on the Non-Proliferation of Nuclear Weapons (1968).

16. Article III of the Treaty on the Non-Proliferation of Nuclear Weapons (1968).

17. The list of 44 nuclear-capable states was derived from a formula set forth in the first paragraph of Annex 2 to the Comprehensive Test Ban Treaty (CTBT). The formula establishes two criteria for inclusion on the list of states required for entry into force of that treaty. The first criterion is that the state must have been a member of the Conference on Disarmament on 18 June 1996. The second criterion is that the state must be included in either the IAEA list of states that have nuclear power reactors or the IAEA list of states that have nuclear research reactors (Annex 2 to the CTBT List of States Pursuant to Article XIV).

18. By April 2001, 160 of 193 states had signed the CTBT. Of the 44 states listed in Annex 2 to the treaty, 3 states had not signed or ratified the treaty (India, North Korea, and Pakistan). A further 8 states from that list had signed the treaty but not ratified it (China, Colombia, Egypt, Iran, Israel, Ukraine, United States, and Vietnam).

19. NPT Review Conference Statement by the delegations of France, the People's Republic of China, the Russian Federation, the United Kingdom of Great Britain and Northern Ireland, and the United States of America, "Five Nuclear Powers Express Strong Support for NPT," U.S. Department of State, 1 May 2000.

20. The Zangger Committee was founded in the 1970s to establish guidelines for the implementation of the export-control provisions of the NPT. The Nuclear Suppliers Group (1974) controls exports of nuclear materials, equipment, and technology. The Missile Technology Control Regime (MTCR) Guidelines were set in 1987, and in 1992 the Warsaw Guidelines were established to regulate transfers of nuclear-related dual-use equipment, material, and technology.

Chapter 4

1. Michael Wines, "Yeltsin Waves Saber at West," *New York Times*, 11 December 1999, A8.

2. David Hoffman, "New Russian Security Plan Criticizes West," *Washington Post*, 15 January 2000, A1.

3. Statement by Director of Central Intelligence George J. Tenet before the U.S. Senate Select Committee on Intelligence on the "Worldwide Threat 2001: National Security in a Changing World," 7 February 2001.

4. James A. Baker III, with Thomas M. DeFrank, *The Politics of Diplomacy: Revolution, War, and Peace, 1989–1992* (New York: G. P. Putnam's Sons, 1995), 359.

5. Scott Sagan, "The Commitment Trap: Why the United States Should Not Use Nuclear Threats to Deter Biological and Chemical Attacks," *International Security*, Vol. 24, No. 4 (Spring 2000): 85–115.

Chapter 5

1. Suo Motu Statement by Prime Minister Shri Atal Bihari Vajpayee in Parliament, New Delhi, 27 May 1998.

2. Statement by Prime Minister Muhammad Nawaz Sharif at a Press Conference on Pakistan Nuclear Tests, 29 May 1998.

3. Public Affairs Office, "Fleet Ballistic Missile Submarines," *Navy Fact File*, United States Navy, 21 September 1999; Walter Pincus, "Questions Raised on Trident Subs," *Washington Post*, 3 January 1999, A22.

4. Colin Powell, *My American Journey* (New York: Random House, 1995), 486.

5. Quoted in Stephen Budiansky and Bruce B. Auster, "Tackling the New Nuclear Arithmetic," *U.S. News & World Report*, 20 January 1992, 38.

6. Ronald Reagan, "Address to the Nation on Defense and National Security," in *Public Papers of the Presidents of the United States: Ronald Reagan, 1983* (Washington, D.C.: Office of the Federal Register, 1983), 442.

7. Patrick J. Sloyan, "Failure to Destroy Scuds Transforms 'Star Wars' Research," *Houston Chronicle*, 24 May 1993, 2.

8. Office of the Assistant Secretary of Defense (Public Affairs), "The End of the Star Wars Era," DOD News Briefing, 13 May 1993.

9. "NewsHour," Public Broadcasting System, 16 August 2001.

10. See Council for a Livable World Education Fund, "National Missile Defense: Ineffective and Costly," Washington, D.C., February 2001, available at: http://www.clw.org/nmd/bmdbrochure.pdf. See also Lawyers Alliance for World Security, "White Paper on National Missile Defense," Washington, D.C., Spring 2000, available at: http://www.lawscns.org/speeches/NMDwhitepaper.pdf.

11. Interview with Secretary Donald Rumsfeld, "NewsHour," Public Broadcasting Service, 16 August 2001.

12. Ibid.

13. Ibid.

14. "Attack on Iraq; In the President's Words on the Bombing: 'It's a Routine Mission,'" *New York Times*, 17 February 2001, A4.

15. For a trenchant commentary on this point and on the shifting rationales for NMD, which continue to shift, see Thomas L. Friedman, "Who's Crazy Here?" *New York Times*, 15 May 2001.

16. "His Magnificent Obsession," *New York Times*, September 5, 2001.

17. Report by Davis E. Sanger, *New York Times*, September 2, 2001.

18. For an in-depth discussion of the foreign-policy implications of Russian nationalism, see Astrid S. Tuminez, *Russian Nationalism Since 1856: Ideology and the Making of Foreign Policy* (New York: Rowman & Littlefield, 2000).

Chapter 6

1. See Khidir Hamza, *Saddam's Bomb Maker* (New York: Scribner, 2000).

Chapter 7

1. Jayantha Dhanapala, "The State of the Global Nuclear Non-Proliferation Regime: 2001," Monterey Institute of International Studies Workshop, Annecy, France, 21 May 2001.

2. NPT Review Conference Statement by the delegations of France, the People's Republic of China, the Russian Federation, the United Kingdom of Great Britain and Northern Ireland, and the United States of America, "Five Nuclear Powers Express Strong Nuclear Support for NPT," U.S. Department of State, 1 May 2000.

3. Ibid.

4. 1995 Principles and Objectives for Nuclear Non-Proliferation and Disarmament and Final Document of the 2000 Review Conference of the Parties to the Treaty of the Non-Proliferation of Nuclear Weapons.

5. NPT Review Conference Statement by the delegations of France, the People's Republic of China, the Russian Federation, the United Kingdom of Great Britain and Northern Ireland, and the United States of America, "Five Nuclear Powers Express Strong Nuclear Support for NPT," U.S. Department of State, 1 May 2000.

6. Ibid.

7. Ibid.

8. The final document and other related materials for the 2000 NPT Review Conference can be found at the Web site for the UN Department for Disarmament Affairs: http://www.un.org/Depts/dda/WMD/nptrevhome.html.

9. "Farewell Radio and Television Address to the American People, January 17, 1961," in *Public Papers of the Presidents of the United States: Dwight D. Eisenhower, 1960–1961* (Washington, D.C.: Office of the Federal Register, 1961), 1036.

10. *Copenhagen*, a play by Michael Frayn, 1998.

REFERENCES

Arkin, William M., and Hans Kristensen. "Dangerous Directions."
Bulletin of the Atomic Scientists, March/April 1998.

Atomic Energy Commission, Department of Defense. "The Effects of
Nuclear Weapons," 1962. Available at: http://www.cdi.org/Issues/
NukeAccidents/accidents.html.

"Attack on Iraq; In the President's Words on the Bombing: 'It's a
Routine Mission.'" *New York Times*, 17 February 2001, A4.

Baker, James A. III, with Thomas M. DeFrank. *The Politics of Diplomacy: Revolution, War, and Peace, 1989–1992*. New York: G. P.
Putnam's Sons, 1995.

Blair, Bruce. "START III, Nuclear War Plans, and the Cold War
Mindset." *Defense Monitor*, Vol. 29, No. 5, 2000. Available at:
www.cdi.org/dm/2000/issue5/start.html.

Budiansky, Stephen, and Bruce B. Auster. "Tackling the New Nuclear Arithmetic." *U.S. News & World Report*, 20 January 1992, 38.

Butler, Richard. *The Greatest Threat: Iraq, Weapons of Mass Destruction, and the Crisis of Global Security*. New York: Public
Affairs, 2000.

Bynum, R. "Somewhere off the Georgia Coast, a Cold War Relic
Rests." *Associated Press*, 21 January 2001.

Canberra Commission on the Elimination of Nuclear Weapons. *Report of the Canberra Commission on the Elimination of Nuclear Weapons*. Commonwealth of Australia, August 1996.

Council for a Livable World Education Fund. "National Missile Defense: Ineffective and Costly." Washington, D.C., February 2001. Available at: http://www.clw.org/nmd/bmdbrochure.pdf.

Eisenhower, Dwight D. "Farewell Radio and Television Address to the American People, January 17, 1961." In *Public Papers of the Presidents of the United States: Dwight D. Eisenhower, 1960–1961*. Washington, D.C.: Office of the Federal Register, 1961.

Hamza, Khidhir, with Jeff Stein. *Saddam's Bomb Maker.* New York: Scribner, 2000.

Hoffman, David. "New Russian Security Plan Criticizes West." *Washington Post*, 15 January 2000, A1.

Lawyers Alliance for World Security. "White Paper on National Missile Defense." Washington, D.C., Spring 2000. Available at: http://www.lawscns.org/speeches/NMDwhitepaper.pdf.

Kennedy, John F. "The President's News Conference of March 21, 1963." In *Public Papers of the Presidents of the United States: John F. Kennedy, 1963*. Washington, D.C.: Office of the Federal Register, 1964.

NPT Review Conference Statement by the delegations of France, the People's Republic of China, the Russian Federation, the United Kingdom of Great Britain and Northern Ireland, and the United States of America. "Five Nuclear Powers Express Strong Nuclear Support for NPT." U.S. Department of State, 1 May 2000.

Office of the Assistant Secretary of Defense (Public Affairs). "The End of the Star Wars Era." Department of Defense News Briefing, 13 May 1993.

Pincus, Walter. "Questions Raised on Trident Subs." *Washington Post*, 3 January 1999, A22.

Powell, Colin. *My American Journey.* New York: Random House, 1995.

Reagan, Ronald. "Address to the Nation on Defense and National Security." In *Public Papers of the Presidents of the United States: Ronald Reagan, 1983.* Washington, D.C.: Office of the Federal Register, 1983.

Sagan, Scott. "The Commitment Trap: Why the United States Should Not Use Nuclear Threats to Deter Biological and Chemical Attacks." *International Security*, Vol. 24, No. 4 (Spring 2000).

Schwartz, Stephen I. *Atomic Audit: The Costs and Consequences of U.S. Nuclear Weapons Since 1940.* Washington, D.C.: Brookings Institution Press, 1998.

Sloyan, Patrick J. "Failure to Destroy Scuds Transforms 'Star Wars' Research." *Houston Chronicle*, 24 May 1993, 2.

Smith, R. Jeffrey. "Clinton Directive Changes Strategy on Nuclear Arms." *Washington Post*, 7 December 1997, A1.

Tikhonov, Valentin. *Russia's Nuclear and Missile Complex: The Human Factor in Proliferation.* Washington, D.C.: Carnegie Endowment for International Peace, 2001.

Tuminez, Astrid S. *Russian Nationalism Since 1856: Ideology and the Making of Foreign Policy.* New York: Rowman & Littlefield, 2000.

Wines, Michael. "Yeltsin Waves Saber at West." *New York Times*, 11 December 1999, A8.

Index

Accidents, nuclear, 33–34
Adelman, Kenneth, 65
Aiken, Frank, 53
Al Sa'adi, Amer, 21
Anti-ballistic missile (ABM)
    programs, 101
Anti-ballistic Missile (ABM)
    Treaty, 29, 36(table), 66,
    108, 143
Arms control
    major arms control
        treaties and agreements,
        25(table)
    means of control, 12
    UN Charter reference to,
        51–52
    U.S. policy, 149–156
    vertical and horizontal
        proliferation, 77
    See also Disarmament

Arms race, 8
    international reliance on
        arms control agreements
        and treaties, 24–29
    NMD as trigger for, 106, 108
    origins of, 121
Arms reduction
    nuclear weapons states'
        failure to reduce, 45
    strategies for, 16
    U.S. and Soviet Union,
        35–44
    U.S.-Russian joint reduc-
        tion, 77–78
Asymmetric deterrence, 89–93
Australia
    CTBT ratification, 64
    Labor government, 65
    NPT review conference,
        47–48, 61

Aziz, Tariq, 19–22, 41–42,
    89–90

Baker, James, 89–91
Bangkok Treaty, 25(table)
Baruch Plan of 1946, 57
Bhutan, 64
Bilateral U.S.-U.S.S.R./Russian
    Nuclear Weapon Treaties,
    36(table)
Biological weapons, 20–21,
    89–90, 112
Biological Weapons Conven-
    tion, 25(table), 128, 154
Blair, Tony, 65
Boost-phase interceptors, 106
Bush, George W., 106, 110–111,
    144–145, 155–156

"Calculated ambiguity," 89–91
CDI. See Center for Defense
    Information
Center for Defense Information
    (CDI), 34
Chemical weapons, 24, 154
    as motives for Israel's
        weapons program, 85
    as rogue state threat, 112
    nuclear response to non-
        nuclear attack, 89–90
    use by Iraq, 63
Chemical Weapons Convention
    of 1993, 25(table), 128
Cheney, Dick, 102

China
    American military targets
        in, 37
    assistance to Pakistan,
        86, 97
    as threat to India, 2
    current state arsenals,
        31(table)
    enforcing NPT obligations,
        133–134
    failure to ratify CTBT,
        159(n18)
    first nuclear detonation, 121
    impact of missile defense
        on, 15
    impact on Russia's post-Cold
        War nuclear policy, 79
    NMD stance, 107–108,
        117–118
    nuclear capabilities, 30
Client statism, 85–86
Clinton, Bill, 64, 106
Cold War
    as key to international
        security, 28
    escalating arms race,
        100–102
    reshaping Russia's post-
        Cold War nuclear stance,
        77–82
    role of nuclear weapons,
        43–44
Colombia: failure to ratify
    CTBT, 159(n18)

Comprehensive Test Ban
Treaty (CTBT), 2–3,
25(table), 60, 62
India's stance on, 63–64, 95
need for U.S. ratification, 152
nuclear-capable states,
159(n17)
signatory states, 159(n18)
U.S. and Russian resistance
to, 39–40, 65
Conference on Disarmament,
159(n17)
Conventional weapons, 8
as alternative to nuclear
weapons, 125
enforcement of treaties
through use of, 131–132
Cost
of maintaining nuclear
stockpiles, 32–33
of NMD, 106–107
Council on Weapons of Mass
Destruction, 134–138, 154
Counter-proliferation, 71–74
Covert proliferation, 11, 87–88,
110–111, 124. See also
Rogue states
Cuba
Cuban missile crisis, 37–38,
44, 100
failure to adhere to NPT, 58
impact on Russia's post-Cold
War nuclear policy, 79
Cut-off treaty, 39

Daniel, Maureen, 112–113
Deterrence, 8–9
as motive for weapons
acquisition, 99–100
asymmetric, 89–93
escalation of arms race
during the Cold War,
100–101
mutual assured destruction,
121
of rogue states, 111–112
unusability of nuclear
weapons, 92–93
U.S. "calculated ambiguity"
policy, 89–91
Dhanapala, Jayantha, 141
Diplomacy, as alternative to
weapons programs,
125–127
Disarmament, 23, 114
addressing elemental
security problems, 125
as goal for non-proliferation
regime, 141–142
first UN General Assembly,
52
NPT extension debates, 47
NPT obligation towards,
56–57
treaty negotiation, 129
Economic conditions
affecting nuclear stock-
piles, 33
dictating U.S. policy, 116

Egypt, 85, 159(n18)
Eisenhower, Dwight D., 18, 156
Environmental Modification
    Convention, 25(table)

Fischer, David, 139–140
France
    bullying tactics at NPT
        review conference, 60–61
    current state arsenals, 30,
        31(table)
    enforcing NPT obligations,
        133–134
    first nuclear detonation, 121
    increasing reliance on
        nuclear weapons, 143
    Putin's overtures to, 79
    support for Israel's weapons
        capability, 84–85

Garcia Robles, Alfonso, 62
Geneva protocol of 1925,
    25(table)
Germany: Putin's overtures to, 79
Gorbachev, Mikhail, 76
Gulf War. See Persian Gulf War
Gurria Treviño, Jose Angel, 64

Haas, Richard, 145
Hague Peace Conferences, 24
Hamza, Khidhir, 123
Hawke, Bob, 65
Hayden, Bill, xvii
Horizontal proliferation, 82, 93

Human history, interpretations
    of, 3–7
Hussein, Saddam, 110–111
    addiction to weaponry,
        19–22
    motives for acquiring
        weapons, 83–84
    Russia's patronage of, 79

ICBM. See Intercontinental
    ballistic missiles
India, 1–3, 11
    arms reduction, 40
    China's nuclear capability, 30
    CTBT ratification, 63–64,
        159(n18)
    development of nuclear
        weapons, 95–97
    emergence as weapons
        state, 67
    failure to adhere to NPT, 58
    first nuclear detonation,
        95–96, 121
    rationale for weapons acqui-
        sition, 84, 99, 113–114
    refusal to sign CTBT,
        159(n18)
    undeclared nuclear-weapon
        state arsenals, 41(table)
Intercontinental ballistic mis-
    siles (ICBMs), 100
International Atomic Energy
    Agency (IAEA), 57–58,
        87, 139

inherent weaknesses in safeguards system, 68–69
Iraq's covert weapons program, 88, 123
nuclear-capable states, 159(n17)
remedy for rogue states, 114
International Court of Justice, 53
International Criminal Court, 145
International law, U.S. bending of, 145
Iran, 11
  as rogue state, 68
  covert weapons development, 59, 87, 124
  NPT review conference, 49
  rationale for proliferation, 113
  remedy for weapons development, 110
  Russia's support of, 79–80
Iran-Iraq War, 62–63
Iraq, 11
  as rogue state, 68
  covert weapons development, 59, 87, 122–124
  disarming Saddam Hussein, 19–22
  justification for weapons program, 41–42, 83–84, 113
  obtaining Russian fissile materials, 80–81

Patriot missiles versus Scuds, 104
remedy for covert weapons development, 87–88, 110–111
Russia's client statism, 85–86
Russia's patronage of, 79
Isolationism, 116
Israel, 11, 113
  arms reduction, 40–42
  bombing Iraq's nuclear reactor, 83, 123
  failure to adhere to NPT, 58
  failure to ratify CTBT, 159(n18)
  first nuclear detonation, 121
  maintaining nuclear capability, 67
  motives for acquiring weapons, 84–85
  NPT review conferences, 47–48
  undeclared nuclear-weapon state arsenals, 41(table)
Ivanov, Igor, 66
Japan: China's nuclear capability, 30

Kashmir partition, 96
KEDO. See Korean Peninsula Energy Development Organization
Kennedy, John F., 44, 54, 100

Korean Peninsula Energy Development Organization (KEDO), 87
Kuwait invasion, 83

Libya, 64, 85
Limited Test Ban Treaty, 25(table)
Loose nukes problem, 80

Marxist theory, 4
McNamara, Robert S., 37–38
Middle East. See Iran; Iraq; Israel
Milosevic, Slobodan, 146
MIRVs. See Multiple, independently targetable reentry vehicles
Missile defense proposals, 103
Missile Technology Control Regime, 159(n20)
Modernism, 3–6
Moral issues: Saddam's addiction to weapons, 20–22
Multiple, independently targetable reentry vehicles (MIRVs), 100–101
Mutual assured destruction, xi, 101

Narcotics traffic, 147–148
National missile defense (NMD)
    continuing research and development, 152
    U.S. rationale for, 103–106, 108–110
NMD. See National missile defense
Non-nuclear weapons states
    national defense equity with nuclear states, 132–133
    NPT objectives and definition of, 54–56, 59
    See also India; Israel; Pakistan
Non-proliferation, 11
    challenges to disarmament goals, 141–142
    reliability of, 12–15
    U.S. rationale for missile defense, 13–18
North Korea, 11
    as rogue state, 68
    covert weapons development, 59, 87, 124
    impact on Russia's post-Cold War nuclear policy, 79
    refusal to sign CTBT, 159(n18)
    remedy for covert weapons development, 87, 110
NPT. See Nuclear Non-Proliferation Treaty
Nuclear Non-Proliferation Treaty (NPT), 7, 25(table)
    agreement to extend, 45–50
    breakdown through NMD development, 118

cheating from within countries, 121–124

dealing with rogue states, 87

disarmament versus counter-proliferation, 71–74

enforcing Treaty obligations, 133–134

India and Pakistan's development of nuclear weapons, 97

India's refusal to sign, 95

move towards disarmament, 57–58

need for strengthening non-proliferation regime, 141–144

nuclear versus chemical and biological weapons, 127–128

nuclear weapons states' desire to extend, 60–62

nuclear weapons states' failure to comply with disarmament, 65–66

responsibilities of weapons states and non-weapons states, 54–56

UN Charter and, 50–54

U.S. obligations to, 146–147

U.S. response to non-nuclear attack, 90

vertical and horizontal proliferation, 77

weapons states' commitment to disarmament, 66–69

Nuclear Suppliers Group, 159(n20)

Nuclear-weapons states, 27–30

action on NPT review conference items, 153

commitment to disarmament, 66–69

current state arsenals, 31(table)

extension of NPT, 45–50

failure to fulfill NPT obligations, 146–147

impact of NMD on, 107

increase in number owing to NMD, 118

move towards arms reduction, 38–39

national defense as motive for weapons acquisition, 99–100

national defense equity with non-nuclear states, 132–133

NPT definition of, 54–56, 59

nuclear-capable states, 159(n17)

preventing global proliferation, 71–74

Nuremberg Trial principle, 53

Nuremberg Trials, 146

Organization for the Prevention of Chemical Weapons, 136
Ottawa Convention, 25(table)
Over proliferation, 11

Pakistan, 11
    arms reduction, 40
    China's assistance to, 86
    emergence as weapons state, 67, 95–97
    failure to adhere to NPT, 58
    first nuclear detonation, 121
    nuclear tests, 96
    rationale for weapons acquisition, 84, 99, 113–114
    refusal to sign CTBT, 159(n18)
    undeclared nuclear-weapon state arsenals, 41(table)
Pelindaba Treaty, 25(table)
Persian Gulf War, 83, 89–91, 102–104, 123
Powell, Colin, 91, 102, 119, 155
Proliferation, 75–93
    by rogue states and terrorist groups, 87–89
    history of, xi–xii
    need for strategies to prevent, 148–149
    origins of the arms race, 121–122
    rationales behind, 34, 82–83
    rogue states and, 113–114

safeguards against rogue states' weapons proliferation, 69–71
    technology shaping security policy, 98–99
    vertical and horizontal proliferation, 77, 82–83
Putin, Vladimir, 76–79

Radiation, as effect of nuclear weapons, 7–9
Rarotonga Treaty, 25(table)
Rashid, Amer, 20
Reagan, Ronald, 37, 103
Reagan administration, 64–65
Reliability, of NMD shield, 106
Religion, as rationale for war, 23
Replacement phenomenon, 26–27
Retaliation, 34, 89–92
Rihab Rashida Taha, 20
Rogue states, 11
    as rationale for NMD development, 104–106, 109–112, 119
    as threat to arms control regimes, 86–87
    consequences of treaty violations, 130
    international concerns over, 27
    verification of compliance, 68–71, 88
    violation of NPT, 122–124

Royal Zoological Society, 140
Rumsfeld, Donald, 105, 108
Russia, 9
    American military targets
        in, 37
    assistance to India, 97
    client statism, 85–86
    cost of nuclear stockpile,
        32–33
    current state arsenals,
        31(table)
    enforcing NPT obligations,
        133–134
    increasing reliance on nu-
        clear weapons, 143
    NMD posture, 107–109,
        118
    reshaping nuclear stance
        after Cold War, 75–82
    U.S. and Soviet/Russian
        nuclear stockpiles, 28–32,
        29(fig.)
    U.S. rationale for missile
        defense, 13–15
    U.S.-Russian arms reduc-
        tion treaty, 152–153
Russia-China cooperation
    agreement, 79

Science: relation to the public
    good, 6–7
Scud missiles, 104
SDI. See Strategic Defense
    Initiative

Sea-based NMD system, 107
Senate, U.S., 65
Shah, Prakash, 95–96
Sharif, Muhammad Nawaz, 99
Single Integrated Operational
    Plan (SIOP), 37
South Africa, 7, 48, 121, 139
South Asia, as new nuclear
    weapons arena, 96
South Pacific Nuclear Free
    Zone Treaty, 25(table)
Sovereignty issues, 2–4
    treaty negotiation process,
        128
    U.S. sovereignty versus
        NPT adherence,
        144–147
Soviet Union
    arms reduction negotia-
        tions, 35–44
    escalation of arms race
        during the Cold War,
        100–102
    failure of the Baruch Plan,
        57–58
    nuclear stockpiles, 28–31,
        29(fig.)
    See also Cold War
Space-based NMD system,
    107
Stalin, Josef, 44, 121
START. See Strategic Arms
    Reduction Treaty
Statism, 85–86

Stockpiles, nuclear
    current nuclear-weapon
        state arsenals, 31(table)
    Russia's deteriorating
        materials, 81
    U.S. and Russia, 28–32
Strategic Arms Reduction
    Treaty (START), 35–38,
    36(table), 66
Strategic Defense Initiative
    (SDI), 103
Sweden, 121
Syria, 85

Taiwan: China's nuclear
    capability, 30
Target list, 37
Technology transfer, 69–70,
    159(n20)
Tenet, George J., 86
Terrorist groups, 88–89, 91–92,
    154–155
Testing
    China's potential resump-
        tion of, 118
    India's first nuclear test,
        95–96
    Saddam Hussein's weapon,
        83
Threshold Test Ban Treaty,
    36(table)
Tlatelolco Treaty, 25(table), 62
Treaties and agreements,
    25(table)

cheating from within, 124
distrust of, 113, 115–116
enforcement of terms,
    122–123, 130–132
international reliance on
    and adherence to, 24–29
negotiation process of,
    127–130
See also individual treaties
Truman, Harry S., 44

Ukraine: failure to ratify CTBT,
    159(n18)
Undeclared nuclear-weapon
    state arsenals, 41(table)
United Kingdom
    bullying tactics at NPT
        review conference,
        60–61
    current state arsenals, 30,
        31(table)
    enforcing NPT obligations,
        133–134
    first nuclear detonation, 121
United Nations
    arms control treaties, 130
    Charter construction and
        the NPT, 50–53
    UN Conference on Disar-
        mament, 63
    UN Special Commission
        (UNSCOM), 84, 123
United Nations Security
    Council, 134

disarming Saddam Hussein, 19–22
lack of NPT enforcement, 133
remedies for rogue states' covert weapons development, 87–88
remedy for rogue states, 110–111
United States, 9
alternatives to NMD for rogue states, 114–115
arms control policy, 149–156
arms reduction negotiations, 35–44
bullying tactics at NPT review conference, 60–61
current state arsenals, 31(table)
diplomatic relations as alternative to weapons defense, 125–127
enforcing NPT obligations, 133–134
escalation of arms race during the Cold War, 100–102
failure to ratify CTBT, 159(n18)
level of commitment to NPT, 142–147
national missile defense and the ABM Treaty, 66

need for leadership in disarmament, nonproliferation, and arms control, 93
rationale for national missile defense, 13–18, 103–106
technology shaping security policy, 98–99
U.S. and Soviet/Russian nuclear stockpiles, 28–32, 29(fig.)
U.S.-Russian relations after the Cold War, 77–82
Universal Declaration on Human Rights, 53
UNSCOM. *See under* United Nations
Utility, of nuclear weapons, 92–93

Vajpayee, Atal Bihari, 99
Verification, of NPT compliance, 40
as deterrent to weapons development and use, 69
as part of treaty negotiation process, 129
inherent weaknesses in IAEA safeguards system, 68–69
of CTBT, 60
rogue state remedies, 88

versus enforcement, 105

Veto procedure, 133–134

Vietnam
    failure to ratify CTBT,
        159(n18)
    impact on Russia's post-Cold
        War nuclear policy, 79

Warsaw Guidelines, 159(n20)

World War II, 24

Yeltsin, Boris, 75–76

Zangger Committee, 159(n20)

Zero tolerance policy, 147–148

Printed in the United States
76667LV00002B/52-57

9 780813 340975